Devon History

Bigbury, Bigbury-on-Sea & Burgh Island

Over **2500 names** mentioned

many with land or tax assessment included

Edited by Jason D C Sullock

To Linda, without whose support this book
would not have been created

and to the Devon Family History Society
who helped me, without condition, from the start of my quest

Introduction

'Nennius', author of 'The History of the Britons' in the Seventh Century, said when he started his book 'I made a heap of all I could find'.

I have chosen a similar approach.

My aim is to make life a little easier and a little less expensive for those of us who are interested in either family or Devonshire history, and who hail from this small corner of the West Country.

The reader will note that I have restricted this book in two ways:

Firstly by geography... I have so much information on the South Hams that if I add in a 'tidbit' from Ringmore, or a 'human interest' story from, say, Aveton Gifford, then, like dominoes, more and more will fall into the text. I have therefore restrained myself to Bigbury and Burgh Island.

Secondly... I have tried to provide details of land occupation wherever possible. This provides an excellent anchor for anyone searching old maps and actually visiting the South Hams.

Finally, I would like to thank all who helped me collate this material.

Should any reader have more information, I would be only too glad... honoured in fact, to add it to the next edition. Anyone who has bought an earlier edition should contact me at the email address below and I will forward an ebook edition free of charge.

You can contact me on jasonsullock@yahoo.co.uk

Enjoy your read...

Jason Sullock, Teesside, England. 2010

Entry from White's Devonshire 1878:

BIGBURY, a parish which includes the village of St. Ann's Chapel, is in Kingsbridge union and county court district Ermington and Plympton petty sessional division, Kingsbridge polling district of South Devon, Ermington hundred, Totnes archdeaconry and Woodleigh deanery.

It had 465 inhabitants (229 male, 236 females) in 1871, living in 99 houses, on 2902 acres of land, and 265 acres of water. Bigbury village is about $1^1/2$ mile from Bigbury Bay, 4 miles south of Modbury, 6 miles from Kingsbridge, and $8^1/2$ from Ivybridge, and is situated on an eminence about 400 feet above the level of the sea, open on one side to Dartmoor, and on the other to the Channel. It is one of the healthiest in England, and gives its name to the magnificent bay lying between the Bolt Tail and Stoke Point, into which the two rivers, the Erme and the Avon, fall.

On the bay are situated no less than nine parishes, all of them containing fine sites for villas, many of them possessing good hard sands, grand cliffs, and other advantages, which will, no doubt, at some future period make this part of Devonshire, now almost unknown, as justly celebrated as Torbay or Mount Bay. With the exception of the Dart, the Avon is the best salmon steam in South Devon. The supply has increased considerably during the last few years, in consequence of the stricter conservancy regulations, and in course of time under improved regulations, adopted with special reference to the locality, it may be confidently expected that the annual take of salmon will be very large. The right of fishing at the mouth of the Avon belongs to the lord of Bigbury manor, it goes with the Court Farm, and is at present rented by John Ellis, Esq., of Aveton Gifford.

The manor was held for nine generations by a family of its own name, and afterwards passed to the Champenownes, Willoughbys, and Pawlets, it now belongs to the Duke of Cleveland and the Dowager Duchess of Cleveland, and they and J.A Pearce, Esq., are the principal owners of the soil.

In the little hamlet of St. Ann's Chapel there still remain traces of the old chapel. At Milburgh was an oratory near a spring. At Holwell is yet in existence the holy well, from which it is called; on the island of St. Michael de la Burgh, now known as Borough Island or Burr Island, was a fisherman's chapel, dedicated to St.Michael. The CHURCH (St.Lawrence), which had become almost a ruin, was rebuilt in 1872 at the cost of about £1200, raised by subscription, the lord of the manor giving £100. It consists of chancel, nave, and side chapel in the Decorated style, and north aisle of Perpendicular date. The tower, which contains five bells, is surmounted by a spire. In a mortuary chapel, now used as a pew by the holder of Court Farm, is a brass in memory of a member of the Arundel family, and a slate monument, with a very quaint inscription in verse, in memory of a husband and wife of the name of Pearce, bearing the date of 1582. The living, a rectory valued, K.B. at £28 7s. 11d., is in the patronage of Lord Sandwich and the Duke of Cleveland, and incumbency of the Rev.F.Farrer, M.A. The tithes are commuted for a rent-charge of £500, the glebe is 100 acres. The BAPTISTS have a chapel here, built about 12 years ago by Mr W. Hooppell.

The parishes of Bigbury, Ringmore, and Kingston constitute the School Board district known as the ERME and AVON SCHOOL BOARD DISTRICT. It was formed in 1873, and now consists of the Rev.F.Farrer (chairman) and Messrs.J. Wroth, W.S. Wroth, John White, P. Randle, Wm. Stidston, and Wm. Hooppell. F.M. Farrer, Esq., is clerk. Existing buildings have been utilized as schools at a nominal rent, in all the three parishes. The three schools will accommodate 200 children, and the average attendance is 170.

1066

Saxon Ordulf holds the manor of Bigbury

1086

Count of Mortain has Manor called Bicheberia which Ordulf held in King Edward's time & it paid geld for 2 hides. 12 ploughs can till.

Reginald De Valletorta holds it of the Count

Reginald has hide in demesne & 2 ploughs & the Villains have 1 hide and 3 ploughs. There Reginald has 12 Villeins & as many Bordars, 1 Rouncey, (unreadable) beasts, 9 Swine, 107 Sheep, 9 Goats, 1 Saltern worth (unreadable) pence a year.

Woodland 1 league in length by 1 furlong breadth, 5 acres meadow & 30 pasture. Worth 60s a year & was worth 7 pounds when Count received it.

[Domesday Book]

'Ordwulf had been Lord of 19 Devon Manors'

[Transactions of the Devonshire Association V & XXVIII]

Bigbury Manor held 9 generations of Bigbury family, then by Champernownes

[Fairweather]

Knightly family 'De Bigbury' lived in adjacent manor house -now Bigbury Court, from the Norman Conquest to 1460.

[Some notes & dates in Bigbury Church & Parish-SI]

John De Bikabery – King John's Reign

[Fox]

1274

Philip De Harwedetone [Harraton] instituted as incumbent of St Lawrences, Bigbury Parish Church

7 February, 1282

Quitclaim

(Notice by Emma formerly w. of Reginald de Remmesbyri she has received 90 marks from Sir Wm. de Bykebiri for marriage of son Reg.). Quitclaim to Wm. De Bykebiri by Emma for above money.

Witd.: Ric. de Boyland justiciar, Gamino de Seccheville, Roger de Prideaus kts., Thom, le Petit, Robert de Pidele parsons, Jn. de Neweton, Wm. de Bykebur de Londesende

Endorsed: "Aquytance of marriage money payed by Sir Willm. Byebury" etc.

Exeter

[ME/818 Cornwall Record Office]

1283

Nativity of John the Baptist, 11 Edw [I]

Lease to farm for 10 years, while in Holy Land

Thomas de Asford, chaplain = (1)

John the clerk, son of (1) = (2)

(1) to (2) his son, all his land in the vill of Asford (manor of Auaton Gyffard); to hold for term of 10 years from the present date, of the lords of Auaton Gyffard; if (1)'s heirs claim the land as their inheritance, they shall give 10 marks silver to (2) at the end of the ten years, and until they do, the land shall remain to (2) and his assigns; but (1), when he returns from the Holy Land, whether within or after the term, shall have the land back as his rightful inheritance.

Nicholas de Cumb', William le Boys, John de Tettawill, William de Harwedaton, Stephen de Hyndeston.

Asford [Ashford, in Aveton Giffard parish, volumes of the English Place-Name Society. Devon 266]

Cumb' [Combe, Aveton Giffard, volumes of the English Place-Name Society. Devon 266]

Tettawill [Titwell, in Aveton Giffard, volumes of the English Place-Name Society. Devon 266]

Harwedaton [sic; Harraton, in Aveton Giffard, volumes of the English Place-Name Society. Devon 266]

Hyndeston [Hingston, in Bigbury parish, volumes of the English Place-Name Society. Devon 267]

[AR/1/1021 1283, 24th Jun Cornwall Record Office]

23 July 1320

Note of judgement in church of Gussinch Regis (?Gussage), Sarum diocese, before Archdeacon of Dorset's Official concerning Sir Jn. Bekebyr and Jn. de Brewes and Rich. le Wolfs (?). Last two bound to Sir J. Bekebyr in 200 marks on marriage between Wm. s. of Sir J.B. and Matilda le Brewes dau. of Giles le Brewes. Sir John takes oath not to give away any part of their lands.

Official binds parties to observe same agreement.

Fragment of seal (eagle) on tag.

[ME/819 Cornwall Record Office]

1325, 19th May

Sir Ralph De Prideaux, Clerk of Bigbury Parish Church. Patron - Sir William De Bikeburi

[Archdeaconry of Totnes]

1332

Robert Chauny, of Challons Combe in Bigbury, listed in Kingston Lay Subsidy

1336

Pilchard Inn on 'Burr' Island built

1342, 19th July

Bykebury

Enquiry made 19th July of the same year. The altar cloths are lost; a surplice is worn out. The processional candles are lost. The belfry is ruinous and badly roofed. There is no manual, the Missal is defective, lacking the week epistles and gospels except in Advent and Lent. The chest for books and vestments is defective; it has no bolt. A nave window lacks glass. A separate Ordinal is needed.

The parishioners are warned.

Sir Ralph, the rector, has done many good things in his time. He has made a new Chancel, sufficiently adequate, and provided new Matins books for the Church. He has built and made many good things for the

Rectory and the Glebe, property repairing the house. He has nothing for the defects.

[Archdeaconry of Totnes]

1343, 7th November

William De Cheverstone, Clerk of Bigbury Parish Church. Patron – Sir John De Cheverstone for William De Bikeburi, a minor

[Archdeaconry of Totnes]

1365

Deed related to farm called 'Frogland'.

Between Richard Wydeslade on one side and Thomas Chonci, Johane his wife & heirs of their bodies on the other.

All messauges, land & tenements which Richard was granted by Roger Chonci of Combe Chonci [Challons Combe] - in Frogghelane & Wodehille.

Witnesses:

William Corbyn

Peter Leye

John Judd

Walter Styna

John De Cumbe

[Cookworthy Museum]

Tuesday 2 November 1361
Grant

1 Wm. de Bykebyr

2 Jn. Chambernon

Wardship and marriage of Alice Jaune by reason of her minority and inheritance she claims in Alyeston in the parish of Modbury (Modbyr). 2 can marry her to whom he will, but to answer to grantor for services and rents belonging to portion of land pertaining to her inheritance. Clause of warranty.

Witd. Wm.Fortescu, Thos Boics, Rich. de Hydeston, Jn. de Combe, Wm. Drake and others.

Seal on tag, circular, black wax, armorial (Bigbury)

Bykebyr Tuesday 2 November 1361

[ME/741 Cornwall Record Office]

Covering dates 4 HENRY IV.

John Drake to grant land in Bigbury to William Poundstock, parson of the church there, and his successors, in exchange for other land in Bigbury, retaining land there. Devon.

[Held by The National Archives, Kew]

1400

Grant (enfeoffment)

1 Wm Bykebury

2 Master Wm Poundstoke; Roger Bachyler; Wm. Chambernou, Jn. Stancombe, Clerk

Manor of Bykebury with advowson and mill and lands etc. in Legh Pevereil, Forsam, Tongyslond and Le Groue. Sealing Clause.

Witd.: Thomas Ferrers; Jn. Drake; Wm. Handyston; Wm. Judde; Wm. Wyrthe

Slit for seal tag.

Bykebury, Monday 8 November 1400

[ME/761 Monday 8 November 1400 Cornwall Record Office]

1402

Grant

1 Wm. de Bykebury

2 Wm. Haukeford, kt., Hen. Foleford, Jn. Chidderlegh and Jn. Gambon, jun.

1's manors of Stonhous, Wythynow and Harebeare with Cremel passage, and all lands etc. in Stonhous, Crymell, Impecombe, Schyndelhale, Anderdonne, Trenyneow, Rodford, Enys, Wythenow, Estharebear, West Harebeare, Cornhele, Smalecombe, Wolmeshyll and elsewhere in county of Cornwall ....

2 seals

Given at Bykebury

[ME/590/1 18 June 1402? Cornwall Record Office]

1412

Letters of attorney

1 Wm. Bykebury

2 Wm. Wenthe

To deliver seisin in (1's) name to Wm. Hankeford, Kt, Henry Foleford, Jn. Chuderlegh and Jn. Gambon jun for their lives.

Manors of Whythenow, Harebeare, Stonhouse (Stonehouse in Plymouth) and Crymel (Cremyll in Rame) with the passage of Crymel.

Part of seal on tag, red wax, poor impression.

Bykebury

[ME/590/2 1 January 1412 Cornwall Record Office]

1414

John Bekebury instituted

1423

Quitclaim

1 Wm. Hankeford, Kt; Jn. Gambon jun.

2 Wm. de Bykebury, Esq.

All manors, knights fees etc. of Stonhouse, Whythenow, Harebeare, passage of Crymel, and lands and app. in Stonhouse, Impecombe, Schynedelhalle, Anderdoune, Trenyneow, Rodford, Enys, Wythenow, Est Harebeare, West Harebeare, Smalecombe, Wolmeshille, which 2 had previously granted to them, together with Henry Foleford and John Chudderlegh then deceased.

Witd: Alex Champernoun; Jn. Dymmok; Robt. Hayes; Jn. Bylhole

Tag for seal (missing); small seal red wax, TW.

Stonhouse

[ME/591 2 November 1423 Cornwall Record Office]

1423

Letter of attorney

1 Eliz. w. of Wm. Bykebury

2 Ric. Uppeton; Walter Palmer

2 to receive seisin of manors of Stonhouse, Wythenow, with passage of
Cremell, Impecombe, Schynedelhall, Anderdoune, Rodford, and Enys,
according to the tenure of a charter by Thomas Stowell, Kt; Wm. Poulet
de Melcombe; Jn. Bykebury, rector of the church of Bykebury; Jn.
Sygnet, clerk; Jn. Gambon, jun; and Wm. Wyrthebo (i).

Circ. seal on tag, red wax; arms, an eagle displayed.

Bykebury

[ME/592/1 Wednesday, 10 November 1423 Cornwall Record Office]

1423

Grant for life of 1's wife, Eliz.

1 Wm Bykebury Esq.

2 Tho. Stowell, Kt, Wm. Poulet of Melcombe, Jn. Bykebury, rector of
Ch. of Bykebury, Jn. Sygnet, clerk, Jn. Gambon, jun, and Wm. Warthe.

1's manor of Stonhouse and Wythenow with Crymell passage and all
lands etc. in Stonhouse, Crymell, Impecombe, Schyndelhalle,
Anderdonne, Trenyneow, Rodford and Enys.

Wits: Alex Champernoun, Jn. Gorgeis, Jn. Dy---, Robt. Hayes, Jn. ---
fole.

Given at Stonhouse

[ME/592/2 10 November 1423 Cornwall Record Office]

1423

Grant

1 Tho. Stowell, Kt, Wm. Poulet of Melcombe, Jn. Bykebury, rector of
Bykebury ch., Jn. Sygnet clk, Jn. Gambon, jun, and Wm. Wertha.

2 Eliz. wife of Wm. Bykebury.

All 1's manors of Stonhouse and Wythenow with Crymell passage and
all land etc. in Stonhouse, Crymell, Impecombe, Schyndelhalle,
Anderdoune, Trenyneow, Rodford and Enys. ...

Wits.: Alex Champernoun, Jn. Gorgeis, Jn. Dymme, Robt. Hayes, Jn.
Bylhole etc.

Given at Stonhouse

[ME/592/3 18 November 1423 Cornwall Record Office]

c1450

Elizabeth, daughter of John Bigberie, marries John Champernown, Knight. His other daughter marries Stephen Durnford.

c1460

Sir William De Begberry, Knight, killed in duel by his cousin Sir John Prideaux of Ordchardton [SI]

Bigbury Manor passed to Champernownes from whom it descended through Willoughbys to Pawleys

1485 (2 Ric [III]); at Westminster
Gift in fee tail

King Richard [III] = (1)

Charles Dynham, esquire for the king's body = (2)

(1) to (2), for his faithful service, especially against traitors and rebels: all lordships, manors, lands, etc., lately of John Halwell, esquire, in Halwell, Westprall, Colatonprall, Combe (in parish of Byggebury), Langeston, Sterte, Westlake, Holbeton, Were in Estyngmouth, Lydeston [sic], Halwell (parish of Halwell), Southpole, Faldepite, Torre in Cornewode (all in Devon), of yearly value of £50; for (2) and his heirs male of his body to hold, together with knight's fees, advowsons of churches, etc., views of frankpledge, hundreds, courts leet, suits, wards and marriages, etc., warrens, wreck of sea, and other profits belonging to them, by knight's service and rent of £3 15s yearly at Easter and Michaelmas. Also all revenues, etc., of the manors from Michaelmas 1483 (1 Ric III).

[contemporary] Memorandum of enrolment of the gift. Seal of (1).

[Devon]

This grant was enrolled: Calendar of Patent rolls 1476-85, pp. 541-42.

Grants of other lands of John Halwell had been made in Aug 1484, to Gilbert Maners and Roger Hertlington: ibid., pp. 478 and 507.

Seal crumbly.

[AR/1/1035 1485, 13th Mar Cornwall Record Office]

Mich. 1494-Mich. 1495
Account roll
Manor of Bigbury:

[ME/1903 1494-1430 Cornwall Record Office]

1495
Manor of Bigbury: Mich. 1494-Mich. 1495 [Manor Accounts?]

[Cornwall Record Office ME/1903 1494-1430]

29 September 1502
Manorial account roll: 29 Sept.

[Cornwall Record Office ME/1916 1501-1502]

1511
Agreement for portion of inheritance of Sir Wm. Bykeby, and counterpart

1 Robt. Willoughby, Lord Broke, cousin and one of heirs of Sir Wm. Bikbury, Kt, i.e. son of Jane, dau. of Elizabeth, wife of Jn. Champernon, squire, one of daughters and heirs of Sir Wm. Bykbury

2 Sir Piers Eggecomb, Kt, and Jane his wife, cousin and another of heirs of Sir Wm. Bikby, i.e. dau. of James Durneford, son of Margt., another dau. and heir of Sir Wm. Bykby.

1 to have manor of Bigbury and advowson there. 2 to have manor of West Stonhouse and lands in West Stonhouse, Withnow, Rodeford, Wynyow, the manor of Westharebeare with lands in Westharebeare, Estharebear, Wilton and Grove, manor of Doddiscombyslygh with advowso of ch. there, lands in Tangiland beside Plymouth, Croketon, Halewyll, Waysshburn, Colaton and Dartmouth, lands in Drake, Howton, Ayleston and Bukland Dynham, lands in Plymouth in possession of Humphrey Talbot and Jane his wife as in right of Jane, cousin and mother heir of Sir Wm. Bykby.

[ME/594/1,2 20 December 1511 Cornwall Record Office]

1507 - 1535
John Cole is Rector . The living is in the gift of Henry VIII

1528

Contemporary copy of an indenture of agreement.

Chas. Blount, lord Mountjoy and Lady Anne, his wife, and John Paulett esq., and Elizabeth, his wife, (Anne and Elizabeth being the daughters and heirs of Robt. Willoughby lord Broke) agree with Francis and Blaunche Dawtrey, Fulke Greville and Elizabeth his wife, [cousins of Robt. Willoughby and daughters and heirs of Edward, Robert's son.]

Property: 1. manors of Broke, Imber and Paxcroft, co. Wilt.

2. Manor and advowson of Pointington, Somerset.

3. Moiety of manor of Tudrington, co. Glouc.

4. Manors of Coppenhall, Fosbroke, Dikron, Robesden, Crakemarsh, and the fair of Penkridge, co. Staffs.

5. Manors of Steeple Mordon and Long Staunton, co. Cambridge.

6. Manors of Claxton and Kilmincoote, co. Leicester.

7. Manor of Cotton, co. Northampton.

8. Manor of Cottred, co. Hertford.

9. Manors of Ropsley, Tothill, Swayton, Helpringham and Frampton.

10. Manors of Hooke, Oberkencombe Chikerell, Thrope Fromevan, Winterbourne and Stepleton, co. Dorset.

11. Manors of Beere Bigbury, Estportelmouthe, Wolstour and Modbury, Devon.

Agreement: 1. The Dawtreys and Grevilles in turn to claim one moiety.

2. Lord and Lady Mountjoy and the Paulets in turn to the other moiety.

3. Remainder in each case to the right heirs of Lord Broke.

Small paper book, 14 pages.

Endorsed Statutum. For Frampton. (Hand of Cuthbert Brereton.)

cf. Anc. V/B/1 supra for similar documents.

[2ANC3/B/27 No date but c. 1528 Lincolnshire Archives]

1541

John Sullock Junior - who holds for the term of his life by copy of court roll that Friday near Feast of St Mark – anno H VIII 7 (1515) one cottage and three acres of arable in common field – fined 24/-herriot paid 5/7d

John Sullock Senior John/Roger sons one cottage and three closes containing four acres – fine 20/-

[11M49/M12 Hampshire Records Office]

Quitclaim relating to a farm called Frogland

William Torryng senior to William Torryng junior, his son – all messauges, lands, tenement etc. in Channecombe [Challons Combe] & Froggelane, & all messauges, lands, tenements etc. in spicers combe, Aveton Gifford.

[Cookworthy Museum]

1542, 21st Mar (33 Hen VIII)

Quitclaim

Anthony Wylloughby de Goreley (Hants) = (1)

Charles Blunt Lord Mountjoy and Lady Ann his wife, daughter of Robert Wylloughby knight, Lord Brooke (deceased), and John Poulet esquire = (2)-(4)

Recites law-suits and contentions between (1) and (2)-(3) in right of (3) with (4) in right of Elizabeth his wife (deceased), the other daughter of Lord Brooke, concerning manors, etc., in Cornwall, Devon, Wiltshire and Dorset.

Quitclaim by (1) to (2)-(4) of all right in the manors of Berefer', Plymmouth, Bigbury, Modbury & Lodbroke, Awnyngmouth & Worthy, Wolston, Est Portelmothe, Hasaworthy, Berealbeston, Berecanteria, Upautry, Raurige, Hempston Arundell, Brixham, Hitcheharundell & Golyworthy (Devon); manors of Kylnodrett & Fursham, Luduanzlez, Trethew, Pendrim, Markewell, Callylond & Callycond, the farm of the works of Saltasshe & Treowen, in Cornwall; the manors of Brouke, Ouercourt, Dylton, Haukryg', Paxcroft, Imber, Westbury, Storiage and Lefyld in Wiltshire; and Hoke, Ouerkencombe, Netherkincombe, Southporton, Northporton, Powerstoke, From, Vowchurche, Westchekerell, Thorpe, Farnesham, Mangarton, Gorewell, Litton, Wythyhoke, Hoshcomb, Winterbornstipleton and Batcombe in Dorset.

Seal; signature of Anthony Wylughby; and of William Shelley at North Gorley as witness. [19th century] Wardour.

Awnyngmouth [= Aunemouth, in Thurlestone, volumes of the English Place-Name Society Devon 312?]

Raurige [Rawridge, in Upottery, Devon]

Hempston Arundell [Little Hempston, volumes of the English Place-Name Society Devon 514]

Hitcheharundell

Kylnodrett/Kylnodred [Poundstock]

[AR/3/595 Cornwall Record Office]

1566

Lease for 80 years

1. Elizabeth Clyff alias Scoble, widow, one of the co-heiresses of Robert Drake late of Bigbury dec., and lately wife of John Clyff alias Scoble, decd.

2. Katherine Gill, lately wife of Roger Gill, and Nicholas and William their sons

Premises: 6 closes called Drakes Grownde and premises held by Johanna Guscott alias Phillipp, widow, late wife of Henry Leigh, for her life

Rent: 20s.

Seal: missing

[2779 M/2/91 1566 Devon Record Office]

1569

Militia List

Devon/Ermington Hundred/Bigburye Parrishe

Presenters sworn

John Strobridge gent

William Burley gent

John Marwood

Who do presente as aforesaid

Thomas Pearse 1 bow, 1 sheaf of arrows, 1 pair of splints

The inhabitants not particularlie chardged by the statute are accessed to fynde and have 2 corslets, 2 calivers

The names of all thabell menne within the saide parishe of Bugburye mustered

Archers

John Stobridge	Richard Riche	John Cooke
Hugh Willinge		

Harquebusiers

John Turpyn	John Baldwyn	Thomas Mooringe
Stephen Parnell	William Plishe	Richard Paige
Simon Coyte	Richard Parnell	Walter Cooke
John Jolle	William Webber	William Nosse
Hugh Wakeham		

Pikemen

George Towson	John Jane	John Giles
John Bytte		

Billmen

John Marrwood	Richard Kitte	John Hache
John Randell	Thomas Pears	John Wakeham
Robert Harwood	John Bowden	John Coyte
Hugh Norrys	John Webber	William Thorne
William Randell	John Forde	Richard Harte
William Shoote	John Ellyott	Thomas Horne
Henry Plishe		

1576
John Sullock registered in Lay Subsidy Rolls

1577
1 Vincent Calmadye, of Wembury, gent and Christopher Martine of Plympton Morrice, gent

2 Edward Hoxte of Middle Temple, gent

Lands etc in Manors of Bigbury and Wheatland

[372/17/4/8 1577 Plymouth and West Devon Record Office]

1582

Pearse – Slate monument in St Lawrence Parish Church

20 February 1587/8 30 Elizabeth I

DIPTFORD

Lease for 99 years determinable on lives.

(1) Beniamyn Taylor of Dipford, yoman.

(2) Thomas Cawley of Greneway, yeoman.

Capital messuage called Farleghe and close called Farlegh parke, both in Dipford, and all other houses, tenements, etc., belonging, (excepting 1 thaked house and 1 herbgarden belonging and 6 closes containing 15 acres, in the occupation of John Burges; one other thaked and a close (3 acres) in the occupation of Christian Campe; a shindle house, stable room, little herb garden and a little plot in the occupation of Nicholas Perrett; the pound meadowe, a little meadow under the long meadow; a little toft and a little beanehaye; with free passage by........the usuall wayes to and from the premises and going of pigges and pultrey

Lives: Lessee, Arthur Strobridge, junior, (son of Arthur Strobridge of Bigbury, gent) and John Milborne, son of Alexander Milborne of Mareldon, yeoman.

Consideration: £500

Rent: £5.

Heriot: Best Beast.

[46/1/4/5 Devon Record Office]

17th Century
Draft lease for 23 years

1 Agnes Pearse of Bigbury, Devon, widow

2 [unreadable]

Moiety of a cottage with appurtenances in Houghton in the parish of Bigbury

[1/642/36 c 17th Century Plymouth and West Devon Record Office]

Date 14 July 1603
Description Will
William Nasse of Bigbury, Devon
[Catalogue reference PROB 11/101]

1606
William Sullicke registered in Lay Subsidy Rolls

1606
Bond for Performance
1 Thomas Burleigh of Bigbury, gent.
2 Thomas Hamblyn
Lease of Waterhead
[1844/3 1606 Plymouth and West Devon Record Office]

1609
William Sullicke registered in Lay Subsidy Rolls

1613
Lease for 99 years or 3 lives
1. Roger Costerd of Aveton Gifford, gent.
2. Thomas Gillard of Bigbury, tailor
Premises: house with a plot of ground attached, a herbgarden next to the house called the Backehouse, all at Fenn in Churchstow, together with commons at Fenn
Lives: 2., Johane his wife and Thomas their son
Consideration: £7
Rent: 2s.
[2779 M/6/2 1613 Devon Record Office]

1617
John Sullock marries Alse Kitt
[Boyds Marriage Index]

February 28th 1619

Bygburye

Mariners and sailors	Age
Robert Burwood	35
Richard Cowkeer	28
Bennet Gross	24
William Hannifer	28
Richard Hatch	40
John Marwood	24
John Peirce	22
John Pless	33
William Sanders	18
Adam Shepheard	28
John Shepheard	33
John Willinge	20
William Yearell	20
Nicholas Yellinge	22

Fishermen	Age
Richard Coyte	45
Nicholas Rundell	38
John Steere	26
John Stone	70

[The Duke of Buckingham's Survey of Mariners and Ships, 1619. Pepys Library, Magdalene College, Cambridge, PL 2122]

1620

Thomas Sulluck was Churchwarden this yer

1626

Robert Cowker marries Rebecca Sullock

1627

Blanch Hust, child Marian, father Ralph Whitchill of Bigbury

[Ugborough 884/277/1 1627]

1627

Assessment for a forced loan

Ermington Hundred (parishes of Ermington, Holbeton, Kingston, Bigbury, Ringmore, Newton Ferrers, Modbury, Aveton Gifford, Ugborough, Harford, Cornwood), with summary for hundreds of Lifton, Tavistock, Roborough and Plympton and parish of Tavistock; divided into lands and goods, with notes about billet money, poverty, absence, default, etc, signed by William Strode, Fra: Glanvill, and Hu: Osborne

[6222 Z/O/1 c.1627 Devon Record Office]

1634, 19th September [written as '10 yr Caroli Primi' or 10th year of the reign of Charles I]

A copy [hold agreement] granted to Thomas Sullock and George Sullock sons of George Sullock for their lives on reversion of him the said George of and in a tenement with portion received 777d

Thomas aged 49 only survivor

[note] George pater mort George fils mort [George the father dead George the son dead]

[HRO 11 M49 Ml3]

1636

Bargain within a marriage settlement

1 William Treeby of Bigbury, yeoman, John Lidston of Ugborough, yeoman and John Cole of Holbeton, yeoman

2 John Rider of Halwill, yeoman, John Lavers of Ashbrenton, yeoman, William Marwood of Bigbury, and John Treeby of Holbeton, blacksmith

Tenement in Bradford, Ugborough

[149/116 20 May 1636 Plymouth and West Devon Record Office]

1636

Bargain and sale

1 Anthony Rous of Halton, Cornwall, esq

2 Thomas Pearse of Bigbury, gent

Tenementas in Loddiswell, West Alvington, Dunstone, Ermington and Modbury

Consideration: £1100

[74/157/17 1641 Plymouth and West Devon Record Office]

26 May 1648

Will of Thomas Pearse, Gentleman of Bigbury, Devon

[Catalogue reference PROB 11/204]

02 August 1652

Will of John Pearse, Gentleman of Bigbury, Devon

[Catalogue reference PROB 11/224]

1653

Assignment

1 Joseph Bastard and George Marke

2 William Bastard

Property in Bigbury

Rent: 3s 4d pa

[74/309/17 1653 Plymouth and West Devon Record Office]

19 May 1653

Description Will of Richard Harris, Yeoman of Bigbury, Devon

[Catalogue reference PROB 11/231]

09 November 1655

Will of Lucretia Perret, Widow of Bigbury, Devon

[Catalogue reference PROB 11/251]

20 January 1658

Will of John Way, Clerk of Bigbury, Devon

[Catalogue reference PROB 11/272]

30 April 1658

Description Will of Jone or Joane Tabb, Widow of Bigbury, Devon

[Catalogue reference PROB 11/274]

1659

Rich. Clarke's house

99 yr lease (lives of lessee; w. Margt.; and Thos., s. of Jn. Tabb of Bigbury); rent 10/-

Consideration: £33

(1) Wm. Gilberd of Sigdon, Charleton, gent., to (2) Hugh Flashman of Kingsbridge, blacksmith

Messuage, tenement, dwelling-house and gdn in Kingsbridge late in occ. of Rich. Clarke

22 Jan. 1659.

[RD/1228 1659 Cornwall Record Office]

18 July 1660

Will of Phillip Tartley, Yeoman of Bigbury, Devon

[Catalogue reference PROB 11/299]

1662

Documents relating to Lord St John, Thomas Pearce, and John Harris – These are counterpart leases for Manor Wood

[HRO ll M49 453]

1662, 1st of September

John Sullock hath this day contracted with the Lord ST John an estate by copie [hold agreement] for the lives of himself and daughter Agnes of and in the same messauge of a copyhold at present in the possession of Elinor Sullock his mother and for another estate by copie [hold agreement] in the other messauge of the same tenement at present which he hath in his possession for his life for the life of John Saunders of Bigbury and he hath now given bond for payment of 60 pounds. Further payments 60 pounds Lady Day and Michaelmas 1663 (paid out the life of John Saunders)

[Note in margin]

By which estate he is to pay a fine of 28 pounds

£loO paid £1 5/-

[HRO llM49 l4]

1664

Documents concerning jointure of Isabel daughter of William, 1st Viscount Stafford.

Manors Ludvan, Pendryn Markwell & Ludvanleaze, Porthia, (except Vuy iuxta Lelant) (co. Cornwall); manors etc. in Hooke and Kencombe, Porton, Batcombe, Chicherell, Poorstocke, Froome Vauchurch, Farnham, Mangerton, Winterbourne, Steepleton (co. Dorset); Bigbury, East Portlemouth, Woolston, Brixham, Hempston Arundell (co. Devon). 1664/5;

Manors of Holshot & Puttham (co. Hants.), 1664, 1672;

St. Margarets, Westminster, house etc. 1680.

These are subsidiary documents of Lord Stafford, and the Marquess of Winchester and Trustees.

[D641/2/B/4 1664-1680 Staffordshire and Stoke-on-Trent Archive Service, Staffordshire Record Office]

1664

Estate Papers - Exemplification of a recovery between William Vise Stafford / Anthony Lord Ashley, and John Marquis of Winchester

[HRO ll M49E/T538]

1664, June

A copy [hold agreement] granted to John Sullock and Agnes his daughter for their lives on reversion of Elinor Sullock in the the moiety of a tenement, one garden and 11 closes of landcontaining 6 acres and 24 acres of arable in the common fields

1665, October

A copy [hold agreement] granted to John Sullock (57) on reversion of John his father in the moiety of a tenement and one farthing of land

[HRO ll M49 Ml3]

1665

Counterpart Lease

1) John Furse of Moorshead, gent., Thomas Hele of Farthell, esquire, and Amy his wife, Thomas Pearse of Bigbury, gent., and Grace his wife (Amy and Grace being the daughters and co-heirs of Agnes Pearse)

2) Richard Turpin of Plympton St Mary, yeoman Field called Higher Preswell, parcel of a tenement in Woodford

Consideration: £28

Term: 99 years or three lives

Rent: 6s 8d pa

[69/M/2/23 4 April 1665 Plymouth and West Devon Record Office]

1666

Reference noted to Edmund Sullock who features in a defamation case with Elizabeth Warren

[Court of Arches]

1667

Saunders surrendered and granted to John son of John Sullock on release of John the father [See entry for 1662]

[HRO 1l M49 14]

1667, 6th May

[John Sullock] £150 given for 2nd Life for both moieties [see entry for Oct 1665]

[HRO ll M49 Ml3]

1671

14 Deeds

Braieswood etc. and Easton

Veale, Goss

[1399M/3/1 1671 - 1787 Devon Record Office]

1678

Samuel Coffin, of Bigbury

[269A/PO 14 1678]

1684

Assignment of lease

1 Lawrence Lang of Ugborough, yeoman

2 Jeffery King of Bigbury, yeoman, and Ralph Lang of Ugborough, yeoman, brother of (1)

Stonehill, Great Halwell, Little Halwell and Halwell

Meadows, Ugborough

Rent: £12 pa

Consideration: £50

[279/110 1684 Plymouth and West Devon Record Office]

1684, 3rd March

[_____] from Mr [_____] Steward [abbreviation unreadable] 2¹/₂ yearly value for additional 1 life to 2 for ye Barton & Nilberwood [or Milerwood] valued at 6 farthings & 7L 8d Margaret estate 25L of farthing

Memorandum to ye Wood and connected lands called Wood Park & Church with hopefully may have been valued with ye Brton

[1lM49/338 Manorial papers 1709-1739 Hampshire Record Office]

1685

Mills - to Samual Woodmason of Bigbury - Labourer

[11M49/338 Mamorial papers l709-1739 Hampshire Record Office]

1685, 5th June

[_____] from Mr Pearse [abbreviation maybe 'regarding'] his land were but 5¹/₂ farthings(of other ¹/₂ farthing being full stated) & hath offered to shew twas worth no more than £20 per farthing – concludes to give £300& not more in any event {if fishery then in a flourishing state}

[_____] out ye Woodpark [?]   at £80

Mansion House   at £220

          £300

Payable at 3 half yealy payments

Valued at 3 farthings) As to Tuffland valued at £55. Mr Pearse has long since let it at £50 payment.

Not worth above £l l0s) Church House – Cottage valued at £2

[11M49/338 Manorial papers 1709-1739 Hampshire Record Office]

1689

[John Sullock] £68 given for 2nd Life for one moiety [sse entry for Oct 1665]

[HRO ll M49 M13]

1693

Tempance Pitwood apprenticed to Nicholas Adams of Bigbury, yeoman

[269A/PO 348 1693]

1693-1694

Presentation of John Edgcombe, M.A., to the rectory of Ringmore, vacant by the death of George Reynell, clerk.

John Fortescue of Holbeton, gentleman, and Mary, his wife, administratrix of Daniel Getsius of Bigbury, clerk, (to whom the advowson belongs this time by virtue of a conveyance of the next advowson by Francis Kirkham of Puicourt Devon, Esq. to Walter Jago the younger, merchant, and a conveyance made by him to Daniel Getsius) to Jonathan (Trelawney), Bishop of Exeter.

(Not executed).

[107/863 -- March, 6 William & Mary, 1693/4 Plymouth and West Devon Record Office]

1694, 12th October

Marriage of John Rotherick of Holbeton and Mary Sullock

1696

Thomas Sullock senior – Jury man

[HRO –Manorial Court Records]

1696, 3rd November

Marriage of Thomas Sullock of this parish and Rachel Serry [?] of Chostow

[Bigbury Parish Registers]

1697

Lease for 99 years

1 Thomas Pearse of Bigbury, gent

2 John Peach of Dunstone, Yealmpton, spinster

Tenement in Dunstone, Yealmpton

Rent: 32s pa

[74/157/1 1697 Plymouth and West Devon Record Office]

1699-1700

Bill of complaint of John Fortescue of Combe in Holbeton, Esq., administrator of Daniel Getsius, clerk, Rector of Bigbury, deceased, to Hon. John Lord Somers, Baron of Evesham, Lord High Chancellor.

Stating that Daniel Getsius, on 5 February, 27 Charles II (1674/5), acquired from Rachel, Countess Dowager of Bath, Lady of the manor, a reversionary lease for two lives of a copyhold tenement in the manor of Kingston, the term to commence from the death of James Watson, clerk, the present tenant, at rent of 22s 8d.

And that the lease was granted to Daniel Getsius and Walter, his brother, Walter having promised to act as a trustee for Daniel, his executors, etc., and that Walter signed a bond to this effect on 16 June 1675.

And that Daniel Getsius died in 1691, leaving no widow, but only Mary, his daughter, who died in her minority, 3 ½ years ago, having. been married to the petitioner 3 ½ years before that.

And that Walter Getsius borrowed £6 from Daniel Getsius shortly before his death, and the money is still owed; and that he took several books, worth about £10 from Mary Getsius, and has never paid for them.

And that Walter Getsius, with the help of James Goodright and others, obtained possession of the copy of court roll, the bond, etc. and now disturb the petitioner and his undertenants, James Wood, Thomas Gilbert, Arthur Courtice, Robert Gilbert senior, James Gest, John Robins, Robert Gilbert junior and John Brooking, in their possession, and has brought pleas or trespass against them all.

[107/864 Hilary Term 1699/1700 Plymouth and West Devon Record Office]

1699, 14th November

Marriage

Robert Nichol of Harberton and Elizabeth Sullock of this parish

[Bigbury Parish Registers]

[The following, unless otherwise stated, are from 11M49/338 Manorial papers 1709 - 1739 Hampshire Record Office]

1699

Deed of trust

1 Thomas Pearse and others

2 William Woollcombe of Plympton St Mary, gent and Andrew Phillips

To administer the estate of Thomas Pearse of Bigbury, deceased

[74/157/18 1699 Plymouth and West Devon Record Office]

24 October 1700

Counterpart lease for 99 years or 3 lives

Lessee: John Cory of Bigbury clerk.

Fine: £532 3s.

Premises: tenements in Disborne with 65 acres, with gross timber for repairs, firebote, hedgebote and stakebote.

Lives: Samuel, John and Sarah, lessee's children.

Rent 16s. 8d., heriot best beast or £3 6s. 8d., to plant 3 oak, ash or elm trees annually or forfeit 3s. 4d. for each tree, to grind at the lord's customary mills in South Brent.

Sig. and seal.

[123M/L358 1700 Devon Record Office]

1702

Marriage Settlement

1. Andrew Laskey, clerk, Moreleigh

Rich. Jackson yeoman, Diptford

2. Alice Cranch spinster, Bigbury

3. Joseph Bastard yeoman, Aveton Giffard

Rich. Cranch yeoman, Bigbury

Consideration: marriage of Rich. Jackson and 2. and £200

Premises: messuage called Cleife with outhouses

[872A/PZ 114 1702 Devon Record Office]

1703
Lease and release

1 Thomas Pearse of Bigbury, gent

2 William Woollcombe of Plympton St Mary, gent

3 Samuel How of Plymouth, beer brewer

Messuage, malthouse and brewhouse in Looe Street

Consideration: £130

[710/134 (a-b) 1703 Plymouth and West Devon Record Office]

1705

John Pearse apprenticed to John King of Bigbury, yeoman

[269A/PO 380 1705]

1708

John Matthews of Modbury, farmer reputed father, Edward Matthews of Bigbury esq. Elizabeth Beare of Modbury, singlewoman, 'now bigg with a base child' £40

[269A/PO 270 1708]

1709

Fishery not worth anything

1709

Mary Pulliblank apprenticed to John Adams of Bigbury, gent

[269A/PO 387 1709]

1709

Sarah Chismin apprenticed to John King of Bigbury, yeoman
[269A/PO 386 1709]

1709

Abigail Wakeham

A poor woman now residing in Modbury. She served an apprenticeship with Nicholas Adams or Bigbury for 5 years. Likely to become chargeable to Modbury. Removal to Bigbury.
[269A/PO 146 1709 Devon Record Office]

1710

Assignment

1. Rich. Langworthy esq. Hatch Arundell
Will. Leigh yeoman, Bigbury
2. Hugh Torkington, chirurgeon, late Modbury
Consideration: 1s.
[872A/PZ 120 1710 Devon Record Office]

1715, 9th December

Survey of the Mannour of Howton [in Bigbury Parish]

Acres yearly value and rents of land at Houghton and Hingston
[DRO 3I6M/ES/6]

1715

[Z1/43/3/2 Militia List]

Devonshire

Ermington Hundred

Bigbury Parish

October ye l9th l7l5:

A return of the yearly vallew of each mans estate within the said parish as followeth

Thomas Pears Gent One man	£50
William Cornish Rector Three men	£150
Thomas Pearse Gent One man	£lo-l5s
Thornas Kitt	£12-los
John Sullock	£12-los
Hugh Wakeham	£6-5s
Mr John Cary One man	£50
Richard Shepherd Gent One man	£40-l2s-6d
Nicholas Rundle	£3-2s-6d
Ambros Elliot	£6-5s
Nicholass Adams One man	£50

Robert Frood   £18-17s-6d
  One man

John Wakeham   £12-10s

James Shephed   £6-5s

William Wotton   £6-5s

Brigit Kitt   £6-5s

Mr Richard Cranch   £20-2s-6d
  One man

John King   £15-12s-6d

John Saunders   £6-5s

John King   £50
  One man

John Cranch   £25
  One man

John Avent   £25

John Treeby   £37-10s One
man

The occuupiers of Phillips estate in Howton   £12-10s

William Leigh   £15-12s-6d
  One man

John Get[?]ins for Duks Mills   £9-7s-6d

The occupiers of Philli & Hewdown   £16-13s-4d

Andrew Phillips   £4-3s-4d

Richard Bardens   £4-3s-4d

Hugh Hingston   £15-12s-6d
  One man

Tabitha Willing   £3-2s-6d

Simon Bardens   £6-5s

Stephen Willing	£6-5s
Joshua Towson	£6-5s
William Gilberd	£12-los
John Harris	£16-l3s-4d
One man	
Stephen Shepherd	£4 [changed
to 3]-3s-4d	
Ambros Elliot	£2-ls-8d
Thomas	£2-ls
Jone Willing	£6-5s
Elizabeth Turtley	£l2-los
George Steer	£6-5s
Nicholas Elliot	£l

The yearly vallew of Estates of the Tinners as followeth

Francis Edwads and Sarah Harris	£22-4s-5d
Benjamin Geech[?] for Bayles	£16-13s-4d

[Signed]

John Sear
Samual Cooke
[Arthur?] Chmpernowne

1716

The presentment of the homage at a Court Barron held for His Grace
the Duke of Bolton the manor of Bigbury the 12ᵗʰ day of May 1716

Imperitous

We present all free holders copy holders and lease holders that have
made default this day and for non appearance and we do [charge] them
three pence a piece

Item we present ye death of Elizabeth [_____] and of James
Hoople the son of Nidolas Hoople the next life

Item we present Thomas Kitt to be Rieve for ve yeare ensuing [next]

Item we present ye Lord & Ambrose Elliot to be stentors for ye grace
ensuing

We whole names here under written doo agree to the abovesaid
[assessment]

Hugh Hingston

Williarn Leigh

Andrew Phillips

Simon Bardons

Nicholas Rindle

Thomas Kitt

Stephen Willing

Richard Bardens

Nicholas Elliot

Ambrose Elliot

John Harris

1718

The presentment of tbe homage at a Court Barron held for His Graace the Duke of Bolton the manor of Bigbury the 23rd day of May l7l8

Imperitous

We present all freeholders copyholders and lease holders that have made default ltis day and for not appearing we do [charge] them three pence each

Item we do present ye death of Agnes Webber & Philip Webber ye next life

Item we present ye death of Jonathon Saunders & ye estate in ye Lords hand & a Swinehog taken for a herriot valued at six shillings

Item we present ye death of John Saunders on Joan Willings estate & Thomas Pearce gent ye next life & that a sheep was taken for a herriot valued at six shillings

Item we present Ambrose Elliot for not grinding at ye manor mill

Item we present John Saunders gent for letting downe his late house [this written through, presumably because he had just died!]

Item we present Jaimes Hupels estate [?] for to do ye office of a reeve of ye year ensuing [Philip Creese Mr]

Item we present Hugh Hingston & Elizabeth Shaw to be stentors for ye year ensuing

We whole names and have underwritten do agree to ye presentments abovesaid,

John Treeby

Jos [Avent]

Andre Phillips

William Lee

John Sullouok

Richard Bardens

Ambrose Eiliot

John Blackler

Thomas Kit

Stephen Shipherd

Thomas Sullock

1720

John Edgcombe apprenticed to John Bevell junior, of Bigbury, tailor
[269A/PO 427 1720]

1720

The presentment of the homage at a court barton held for Lord Grace
the Earl of Bolton Manor of Bigbury this 28th day of May 1720

Imperitous

We present all freeholders copyholders & lease holders that have made
default this day & for not appearing we do [charge] them three pence
each:

Item We present Richard Shipherd gent being dead & that a [baliffe?] is
due & his son Arthur ye next heir now to be taken tenant [this last
written through]

Item we present ye death of Ambrose Elliot & his wife ye next life by
virtue of her widowhood & that there is too herriots due for ye one was
taken one sheep valued in six shillings, & for the other one swinehog
valued in [five & six pence]

Item we present Thomas Elliot for not grinding to ye lords mill

Item we present John Sullock for not grinding to ye lords mill

Item we present John Avents tennant Thomas Elliot for not grinding to ye lords mill

Item we present his grace the duke of Bolton to be reeve for ye year ensuing

Item we present Thomas Kitt to be stentor for ye year ensuing and also Mary Wakeham:

We whole names and have underwritten doe agree to ye abovesaid presentments and witness our hands

Joseph Avent

Andrew Phillips

William Leigh

Jonathon Sullocke

Hugh Hingston

Thomas Elliott

Nicholas Rindle

Stephen Shipherd

John Blacklor

1721

The presentment of the homage at a court baron held for his grace the Duke of Bolton Manor of Bigbury this 27th of May 1721

Imperitous

We present all freeholders copyholders & leaseholders that have made default this day & for not appearing wee doe [charge] them three pence each

Item we present ye death of George Sherrif freeholder & his son ohn ye next heire & a releife due to the lord

Item we present ye death of William Leigh &Jean his wife the next life taken for her widowhood now to be taken tenet

Item we present the death of Francis Coker

Item we present Thomas Pears: gent: for letting downe of his house at Town Gate

Item we present Mr John Sullock to be Reve for ye year ensuing

Item we present his grace the Duke of Bolton & Joan Willing to be Stentors for this yer ensuing

We whole names are hear under written doe Agree to ye Abovesaid presentments

Jos Avent [very very shaky handwritting]

John Sullock

Hough Hingston

Richard Bardens

Nich Rundel

John Blackler

James Sheperd

Thomas Elliott

William Leighe

1722

Susannah Cocker singlewoman

Last legally settled in Modbury by her having been bound and serving as an apprentice with Mr John Cranch in Modbury. Now resident in Bigbury and chargeable there. Removal from Bigbury to Modbury.

[269A/PO 117 1722 Devon Record Office]

1722

The presentment of the homage at a Court Baron held for Lord Grace the Duke of Bolton the Manor of Bigbury this second day of June 1722

Imperitous

We present the freetrolders copyholders & lease holders that made default of appearance at this court & do [charge] them 3d each

Item we present the death of Ffrancis Edwards a leaseholder of this manor & the estate is the Lords lands & a herriot] due to the lord

Item we present Ralph Larkman for the making of an encroachment on the Lords lands & planting of food & cutting [_____]

Item we present Joane Willing for letting the wall of the house to be out of repaire

JW [Initials] ordered that she repaire the wall by the next court on the penalty of 3&4d

Item we present that Gent Thomas Pearse hath not repaired the house at the Town Gate which was presented the last court.

Item we present Stephen Willing to be reeve for the next year ensuing

Item we present John Sullock & Hugh Hingston to be Stentors for the year ensuing

Hugh Hingston
Andrew Phillips
Richard Bardens
Thomas Elliott
John Blackler
Thomas Sullock

Thomas Kitt

Nicholas Eliott

Richard Keett

1723, 13th August

Marriage of Thomas Sullock and Joan Willing by banns

[Bigbury Parish Registers]

1723

The presentment of the homage at a Court Baron held for Lord Grace
the Duke of Boltons Manor of Bigbury this ffirst day of June 1723

Imperitous

We present all freeholders copyholders & leaseholders that have made
default this day & for not appearing we do [amerce? Charge?] them
three pence each

Item we continue the presentment with Ralph Lakeman

Item we present the Reverand Mr Cornish for making an encroachment
upon the Garden belonging to the mannor mill

Item we present Mr John King for debarring ['_____people of
written out] several families to ride their Church parth being a [Leach?]
way over a field called Windeat & a lawful parth well known by all the
parishioners

Item we present Mr Anthony Cornish for not grinding to the mill

Item we present Mr Pearce as the last year

Item we present Richard Bardons to be Rieve for the year ensuing

Item we present Joshua [Tomsens?] & Stephen Willing to be Stentors
for tbe year ensuing

We whole names are here underwritten do agree to the abovesaid
presentment

Hugh Hingston

Joseph Avent

Andrew Phillips

John [Griffins?]

William Leigh

Joshua [Thomson?]

Thomas Sullock

Richard Bardens

Thomas Elliott

Nicholas Elliott

Richard Kitt

John Blackler

Ambros Elliott

1724, 26th December

Marriage of Phillip Trennick and Agnis Sullock by banns

[Bigbury Parish Register]

1725

The presentment of the homage for the mannor of Bigbury at a Court
Baron held there for his Grace Charles Duke of Bolton the 22nd May
1725

Imperimos

We present all ffree holders and coppy holders that have made defalt
this day and we made them [charge?] 3 pens each

Item we present Gefferey King [Dengell?] by the informashon of Richard Peas Mellere [Miller] for kiping the watter from the mill

Item we present Richard Woodmason for kiping of the watter one a [_____] Lords Land

Item we present Thomas Eliott Gent to be reef for the year insuing

Item we present Hugh Hingston Gent and Thomas Eliott Gent to be Stentors for the year insuing

Witness our hands hear unto

Hugh Hingston

Thomas Elliott
John Sullock
Richard Bardens
Nicholas Rindell
Stephen Shephard
Nicholas Eliott
Thomas Sullouck
Richard Keett

1726

The presentment of the homage of the Mannor of Bigbury at a Court Baron held the 4th Day of June 1726

Item we present William Ellare Esquire ffree tenet deseased and a retern [of Don?] to the Lord

Item we present Jams Phillips Lese Houlder deseased and the estat fell to the lord

Item we present Thomas Sallouck for letting down the out hous & that it be repaired by [something written through...looks like Michal. Possibly Michalmas] next on the penalty of 20d

Item Richard Pease the Mellere [Miller] presented William Hugh for not grinding att the mill and Like wise for [damming?] the watter from the Lords Mill & doe [charge] him 3s:4d

Item Richard Pease the Mellere [Miller] presented William Stear for [damming?] the watter from the Lords Mill and Likewise for not grinding att the mill

Item we present all free houlders copyholders and Lese Houlders for making defalt this day and [charge] 3d pens each

Item we present William Colton for to be Reef for the year insuing & Brigett Keetts Estate

Item we present Hugh Hingston and Thomas Eliotto be Stentors for the year Insuing

Hugh Hingston

Richard Bardens

Nicholas Rendell

Nicholas Eliott

John Sullock

Steven Shephard

Thomas Willing

Richard Kitt

1727, 23rd May

Marriage of Thomas Sullock and Joan Reeve

1727

The presentment of the homage at a Court Baron held for the Mannor of Bigbury the 27th day ofMay 1727

Impirmis

Wee present all freeholders & copyholders which have made default this day & wee make ich of them six pennes

Item we ['present' crossed out] ye death of William Ellert Esquire & a releaf due to the Lord

Item we present ye death of Bridget Kitt widow & Joan Wotton to be the next life

Item we present Elizabeth Steers Estate for to doe ye ofiss of a Reefe for ye year ensuing & William Colton appointed for the same

Item we present Thomas ['Kitt' written out] Sullock & ['Joan Wotton' written out] William Wotten for to bee Stentors for ye year ensuing

Hugh Hingston

William Lees

Richard Bardens

Nicholas Rendell

John Sollock

Thomas Elliott

Stephen Sheperd

Thomas Willing

James Sheperd

1728

The presentment of the homage at a Court Baron held for the Mannor of Bigbury the 8th day of June 1728

Imprimis

Wee present all freeholders & Coppiholders which have made default this day & wee make [charge?] them each three pence

Item wee present Nicholas Adams for stopping ye water for comeing to ye Lord Mills by ye informaison of ye Richard Pease ye miller

Item wee present your lordducks estate to doe ye office of a reefe [_____] for ye yeare ensuing & William Colton sworne accordingly

Item wee present Hugh Hingston & William Colton for to be Stentors for ye year ensuing

Hugh Hingston

Thomas Sullock

John Blackler

Thomas Elliott

Thomas Willing

John Sullock

Nicholas Rundel

Richard Bardens

1728

Christopher Woolridge apprenticed to John Woolridge of Bigbury, yeoman

[269A/PO 468 1728]

1728, 29th September

Marriage of George Sullock and Mary Lakeman

[Bigbury Parish Registers]

1729

The presentment of the homage at a Court Baron held for the Mannor of Bigbury the 31st day of May 1729

Imprimus

Wee present all freeholders, coppie holders & leaseholders, for not appearing heare this day, wee ['mars?' charge?] them three pence each,

Item wee present the death of Christian Elliott, & Thomas Elliott the next life, ['& a swinehog taken for a heriot allowed' this written through]

Item wee present ye death of Elizabeth Sture & ye estate fallen in ye Lords hand

Item wee present ye death of Richard Kitt, & his widow [?] Kitt, the next life for her widowhood

Item wee present John Harris, his estate for dowing ye office of a Reve,for ye year ensuing,

Item wee present [Turlleys?] estate, which is in ye Lords Land, to be Stentor for the year insuing,

William Lee

Johnn Sullock

Richard Bardens

Nicholas Rendell

Nicholas Elliott

Thomas Elliott

John Blacker

Thomas Willing

Randel Reefe

1730

Lewis White apprenticed to Jeffery Kingdingle of Bigbury

[269A/PO 480 1730]

1730

The presentment of the homage at a Court Baron held for the Mannor of Bigbury the 23rd of May 1730

Imprimus

Wee present all free Holders Copy Holders & Leass holders for not appearing heare this day wee [mars? Charge?] them three peance each

Item we present the death of John Treeby & his wife Elizabeth the next life for her Widowhood

Wee present the death of Ambros Elliott, and John Elliott the next life

Item wee present ye death of Magery Webber & Mary Brend ye next life

Item wee present Thomas Kitts Estate & Mary Wakehams Estate, to be Reves for ye year Insuing & William Colton sworne accordingly

Item wee present Nicholas Rundle & George Sullock to be Stentors for the year insuing

Hugh Hingston

William Lee

Thomas Elliott

Richard Bardens

Nicholas Rundle

Randle Reve

John Blackler

1731

The presentment of the homage at a Court Baron held for the Mannor of Bigbury the 12th day of June 1731

Item wee present all free holders & coppie holders for not appearing here this day wee [mars? Charge?] them three pence each

Item wee present Thomas Elliott for making dung in Richard Bardons pott water,

Item wee present Sanders tenenment being now in our Lord Dukes hand, & Thomas Sullock Senior, to be the office of Reve [_____] for this year,

Item we present Thomas Kitt & Nicholas Rundle for his sisters tenenment,to be Stentors this year,

Hugh Hingston [Very very shaky hand]

William Lee

Richard Bardens

Randle Reve

Nicholas Elliott

James Shiphard

John Blackler

1732

Aaran Woollridge apprenticed to John Woollridge of Bigbury, butcher

[269A/PO 496 1732]

1733

Counterpart lease for 99 years

1. Hugh Stafford, esq., Pynes

2. John Finney, clerk, Bigbury

Consideration: £39 - 11s.

Premises: one undivided third part of houses, rooms, gardens, closes, all of which formed the undivided moiety of Fosters Tenement at Blagdon

[872A/PZL 22 1733 Devon Record Office]

1733

Moiety of tenement late Simon Barden's. (Towson)

[D/MAP/T114 1733 Dorset History Centre]

1733

Release (lease for a yr missing); consideration £250

(1) Jeffery King Dingle of Bigbury, Devon, gent., to (2) Eliz. Sheere Linkinhorne, spr.

Houses in Clampit or East Clampit late in occ. of Wm. Sheere, great-grandfather of lessee, with fields (named) and commons in townplace and moor

21 Apr. 1733.

[RD/574 1733 Cornwall Record Office]

1732, 13ᵗʰ June

Computation of present value of manor of Howton

Names of Tenement - Gertrude Adams Formerly Armorel Elliot's

Yearly value - £21/10/00

Rents - 15/02

Neat value - £20/11/10

Amount of neat value at 21 years purchase - £432/08/06

Lives in being and their value - Thomas Sullock (63), Thomas Adams (44), Gertrude Adams (48)

Value of rend in ffee - £205/10/04

Value of reformed rents at 25 years purchase - £22/14/02

Heriots best beast or - £3/06/08

At 11 years value - £226/10/02

[Ditto 10 Dec 1715]

[The following have no date but clearly belong with the above entry in time as they concern the same land holding]

Armorel Elliot's Tenement

All that messauge and ½ ffarthing of land late in ye tenure or occupation of Thomas Sullock the elder his assigns or undertenant and now in ye tenure or possion [as written] or occupation Armorel Elliott, her assignee or assigns or undertenant being the moiety of halfendeale of one ffarthing of land situate lying and being within ye parish of Bigbury and part of the mannor of Hoghton there sometime howtofore in ye possion of William Elliott

William Elliotts now called Armorel Elliotts and Gertrude Adams tenant to moiety of it

[DRO316M/ES/10]

1732

The presntment of the homage at a Court Baron held for the mannor of Bigbury the 27th day of May 1732

Impris

We present, all free holders coppy holders & leas holders for not appearing heare this day we [marss? Charge?] them tbree pence each

Item we present the death of Elizabeth Bardens, and the estate fallen in the Lords hand, a herriot taken valued in nine shillings

Item wee present the death of John Harris Gent

Item wee present John Sullock Junior? To be Reve for the year insuing

Item we present Sanders Tenenment, being now in his Grace ye Duke of Boultons hand, and Thomas Sullock Senior to be Stentors for the year insuing

Hugh Hingston [handwriting smoother than previous year, suggesting he had been ill previously]

William Lee

Nicholas Elliott

Nicholas Rundel

Steven Shepherd

Thomas Willing

Randel Reve

1733

The presentment of the homage at a Court Baron held for the mannor of Bigbury the nineteenth day of May one thousand seven hundred and thirty three

Imprimis

Wee present all freeholders & coppiholders which have mad edefault this day and wee [mas? Charge] them pence eich of them

Item wee present the death of Elizabeth Shaperd and the house in ye Lords hand

Item wee present the death of Randel Reefe & his wife to be the next life for her widowhood

Item wee present Thomas Sullock and Thomas Elliott to bee Stentors for ye year ensuing

Hugh Hingston

Thomas Elliott

Nicholas Rundel

Thomas Willing

James Sheperd

Richard Bardens

Stephen Shephard

1734

Mortgage

Mary Dyer to Mary King,

Bigbury, and her trustee

Kerse tenement, South Milton

To secure: £200 on 2000 year term

[1768M/T/29 1734 Devon Record Office]

1734

The presentment of the homage at a Court Baron held for the Mannor of Bigbury the first day of June 1734

Item wee present all copyholders ffree holders and leaseholders that have made for default this day and wee [mas? Charge?] them three pens each

Item wee present Mr Arddam Sweet ffee holder deed and Mr [_____] Sweet the next [_____] and a relief due to the Lord

Item wee present Margatt Lee to be daed [as writen] and that house no in the Lords hand

Item wee present Thomas Sallouck to be deed and Joan Sallouck the next line by her widdowood

Item wee present John Blackler to be deed Richard Trennick to be the next line

Item wee present Deborry Steers for not grinding att the mannor mill

Item wee present Nicholas Eliott for not grinding att the mannor mill

Item wee present Andrew [_____] to be deed and a herriott due to the Lord

Item wee present Mr Thomas Pease Junior to be Reef for the year insuing

Hugh Hingston

Richard Bardens

Thomas Willing

Soloman Rider

Nicholas Rinddell

James Sheperd

1735

Mortgage

1 William Dyer of Middlesex, esq, and Joseph Biscoe of London, gent

2 Thomas Borrett of London, esq

Rectory and Tithe Egg Buckland, premises at Yealmpton, Bigbury and Modbury

[567/64/6 1735 Plymouth and West Devon Record Office]

1735

Moiety of tenement, a farthing of land (3½ acres), and 17 acres on Bigbury Down called Copped Furze. (Sullock).

[D/MAP/T115 1735 Dorset History Centre]

27 September 1735

Letter from John Pollexfen to John Fortescue, agreeing to the withdrawal of presentments against the parishes of Bigbury and Kingston, for failing to repair the road between Modbury and Kingsbridge.

[Devon Record Office 48/26/10/22 27 September, 1735]

1735

The presentment of the homage at a Court Baron held for the Mannor of Bigury the 24th day of May 1735

Imprimus

We present all free holders Coppie holders & lease holders for not appearing have this day we [mars? Charge?] them three pence each

Item wee present the death of Mary Wakeham widow and the estate fallen in the Lords hands

Item we present the death of William Cornish and the estate fallen in the Lords hands

Also we present William Lee to serve the office of Reeve for the year ensuing for Mary Avents Estate

Wee doe all agree to the abovesaid presentments

Hugh Hingston

William Lee

Richard Bardens

Thomas Elliott

Soloman Rider

Thomas Willing

Nicholas Rendel

Richard Trinnick

James Sheperd

Stephen Shepherd

1736

Mortgage for £150 + interest (assignment of lease)

1 Thomas Adams of Bigbury, yeoman

2 Robert White of Kingsbridge, cordwainer

A tenement and ½ farthing of land (about 23½ acres) and the moiety of a tenement and field called Dutch End Park (about 24 acres) Both in the parish and manor of Bigbury

Endorsed: "Leasehold expired"

[1076/4 1736 Plymouth and West Devon Record Office]

1736

Mary Tennis apprenticed to Jeffery Kingdingle of Bigbury, yeoman

[269A/PO 522 1736]

1736

The Presentment of the homage at a Court Baron held for the mannor of Bigbury the 11th day of June 1736

Imprimus wee present all freeholders and coppi holders that have made defalt this day wee eich of them three pencs

Item wee present ye death of [_____] Swete a free holder and a relief due to the Lord

Item we present ye death of John Solock and two herriots due to the Lord

Item wee present the death of Nicolas Elliott and ['a herriot due to the Lord' this last written through]

Item wee present ['Geffere King' this written out] ['Antony Cornish' this written out] Thomas Kitt to Reefe for this yeare

Hugh Hingston

Thomas Elliott

Richard Bardons

Thomas Kitt

Solomon Rider

Richard Trennick

Jams Shiphard

Stephen Shiphard

1736, 15th July

Marriage of William Sullock and Elizabeth Whidon by banns

[Bigbury Parish Registers]

1737

Moiety of a farthing of land (3½ acres), Little Field at Sedgwell, and field called Yarden (or Yonder) Furze. (Adams, Yabsley, Kerswell).

[D/MAP/T117 1737-1809 Dorset History Centre]

1738

The presentment of the homage at a court baron held for the mannor of Bigbury the 26th day of May 1738

Inprimis wee present all freeholders and coppiholders and which have made default this day and wee mass [charge?] them eicb, three pence

Item wee present ye deafh of John Elliott and ye tenement in ye Lords hand

Item wee present ye death of Elizabeth Stear and John Pomeryto be the next life

Item wee present Thomas [unreadable] to doe ye offise of of [as written] Reefe for ye year ensueing for Sanders tenement

Witness our hands

Hugh Hingston

Thomas Elliott

Richard Bardens

Stephen Shephard

James Shepard

Thomas Willing

Nicholas Rundel

1739

John Hawkings apprenticed to William Lee of Bigbury, for Mr Rhodes tenement called Hubston

[269A/PO 536 1739]

1739

The presentment of the homageat a Court Baron held for the manor of Bigbury the 8th day of June 1739

Imperimas[?]

Wee present all freeholders coppiholders & lease holders for not appearing here this day we [charge] them three pence each

Item we present Thomas Sullock to be reve for the year insuing & Thomas Kitt sworne

Hugh Hingston

Nicholas Rundle

Stephen Shepherd

Richard Bardens

Thomas Elliott

Richard Trinick

11th day of June 1736

Bigbury sail roll

The following list appears to be a roll call of freeholders, copyholders and leaseholder tenants. It certainly dates to before the court baron of 11th day of June 1736 as it is recorded in that court baron that John Sullock, who is listed below, had died.

Thomas Long Esquire

Adrian Sweet Esquire

Mr Harry Lotting

Mr Arthur Shepardes

Heirs of Ellis Heale Esquire

William Elbert Esquire

William Choldwilth

John Cranch

John Sherrow

Evans Cove Esquire

Tennants of Howton

      Copy and Lease holders

Mr Thomas Peace

Mr William Cornish [written through]

Mr John Cranch

Mr John Harris

Anthony Cornish

John [written through] Elizabeth Treby widow

James Phillips [written through] Anthony Cornish

[something writtur through] Tohmas Elliotts

William Loe

Thornas Kitt

James Shepard son

Stephen Shepard

Richard Barden

Hugh Hingston

Tabitha Willing

Nicholas Rundell

Marganatt Lee

Mary Avent

      Willing [written through]

Elizabeth Steer

Elizabeth Shepard [written through]

James Shepard [son]

Elizabeth Bardens [written through]

Joan Willing

Elizabeth Hardwood [written through]

Nicholas Elliott

Mary Wakeham

John Sullock

Thomas Sullock

Thomas Elliott

Richard [written through] Phillis Kitt

Margery Webber [written though and replaced with] Mary Brend

Joshua Souvent

John Blackler

Philip Webber [witten through]

Joane Pomerry

Ambross [written through] Jonn Elliot

Randell [written through] widow Reve

Thomas Willing

John [written through] Geffery King of Dingle

Richard Barnes

Jonathan Square

Mary King

[Dorset County Records Office - Ref D45]

1740

Cottage and garden late John Elliott's. (Elliott).

[D/MAP/T118 1740,1769 Dorset History Centre]

1740

Lease and release

1 Elizabeth Grove of Wiltshire, spinster

2 Thomas Grove of Wiltshire, esq, Thomas Fane of Bristol, gent, William Hinxman, clerk, and Richard Lamborne of Wiltshire, merchant

Premises at Yealmpton, land at Bigbury, Rectory and Tithes of Holbeton, Egg Buckland and St Budeaux

[567/64/7a and b 1740 Plymouth and West Devon Record Office]

D/MAP/T119 1743

Dorset History Centre

Cottage and 2 acres late John Pomeroy's, and Cott Down Close. (Reed).

1743

Two fields called Cott Parks. (Elliott).

[D/MAP/T120 1743 Dorset History Centre]

1743

House, garden and little orchard late Joan Sullock's. (Reeve).

[D/MAP/T121 1743 Dorset History Centre]

1746

Lidgate Field. (Elliott).

[D/MAP/T122 1746 Dorset History Centre]

1748

Lease for Year

Braieswood

Hammond and others to Veale

[1399M/3/6 1748 Devon Record Office]

l748, 29th August

Ann Harris, widow -tenant to a cottage and garden to hold for her widowhood.

Mary Kit, widow was also admitted as a tenant.

The death of Stephen Sheppard since the last court

William Lee and Thomas Willing 'for not grinding at the Lords mill as according to custom'

[Dorset County Records Office - Ref D45]

1749, 14th August

at this court came Mary Rundle, widow of Nicholas Rundle admittes as tenant to one cottage and five acres of land.

Tabitha for not repairing her ban.

[Dorset County Records Office -Ref D45]

1749

Cottage and three closes of land containing 4 acres. (Foot).

[D/MAP/T123 1749,1805 Dorset History Centre]

1749

Mary Glubb apprenticed to John Chubb of Bigbury

[269A/PO 597 1749]

1750

Thomas Gee apprenticed to John Chubb of Bigbury

[269A/PO 601 1750]

1750, 1st September

Death of Mary Rundle, widow

Death of Mary Kitt. Eleanor Coulton (formally Eleanor Kitt) to be the Lords next tenant.

[Dorset County Records office - Ref D45]

1751, 25th August

George Kingston - Yeoman aged 54 years his son aged 8 years and his sister aged 50 years to pay rent of 10shillings and 8 pence halfpenny per year for one cottage.

1751

The death of Deborah Creer a tenant of the manor.

[Dorset County Records Office - Ref D45]

1752

Moiety of messuage, 4 acres of land and Gubbens field. (Elliott).

[D/MAP/T124 1752 Dorset History Centre]

1752

Cottage and 5 acres. (Borryer).

[D/MAP/T125 1752 Dorset History Centre]

1752, 25th September

The death of Richard Sherriff - a freehold tenant

Death of Hannah Shepherd, widow a copyhold tenant. Thomas Shepherd to be the Lords next tenant.

[Dorset County Records Office - Ref D45]

1753, 8th September

The Death of Thomas Pearce

The Death of Mrs Judith Pearce

The death of James Lamb

[Dorset County Records Office - Ref D45]

1754, September

Death of Joan Wootton a copyhold tenant for the manor

The death of Tabitha Willing a copyhold tenant of the manor

Death of Phillis Kitt - tenant of the manor for her widowhood

[Dorset County Records Office - Ref D45]

1754, 25th September

Marriage of Peter Crocker and Martha Sullock by banns

[Bigbury Parish Registers]

1755, September

We present and continue all former persuements not rectified and amended

[Dorset County Records Office - Ref D45]

1756

Eleanor Ford wife of William Ford (late Eleanor Wootton) was admittd tenant for her life

The death of Helen Coulton. Eleanor Ford being the Lords next tenant

Death of Thomas Long Esquire, freehold tenant of the manor

[Dorset County Records Office - Ref D45]

1756

Particulars, rentals and surveys of estates formerly of John Specott Long of Penheale

Divided between Chas.Davie, Chas.Phillips and Eliz.Long., incl. manors of Penheale, divided between Chas.Davie, Chas.Phillips and Eliz.Long, incl. manors of Penheale, Launceston Lands, Lansallos, and lands In Tresmeer, North and South Petherwin, Jacobstow, Egloskerry,

Tremayne, Laneast, Warbstow, Mary Week, Hollacombe, Holsworthy, Rosecradock, Trewoorick, St.Cleer, St.Neot, St.Winnow, Lantwey, Bodmin, Lewannick, Cardinham, Davidstow, St.Cleather, Rocombe Hugh manor in Stokeinteignhead, St.Sidwells Exeter, Bigbury, Modbury, Chestow, Kingsbridge, Chestas, West Alvington, Dodbrook, North Huish, Loddiswell, Woodley, Aveton Gifford, Marlborough, in Cornwall and Devon, with Lansallos land and window tax 1756.

[DD\DP/82/5 c.1756-79 Somerset Archive and Record Service]

1757

Mr William Cornish for not repairing his house

[Dorset County Records Office - Ref D45]

1758

Dowager Duchess of Bolton dies

Death of Richard Bardons. His widow Mary to be the next tenant for her widowhood.

During the month of October last a ship laden with foreign brandy was wreaked on Borough island otherwise known as St Michaels island within the manor. If no claims be made within a 12 month and a day then the said wreak becomes the right and property of the Duchess Dowager of Bolton, Lady of the Manor.

[Dorset County Records Office - Ref D45]

1758, 31st August

William Coulton and Agnes Sullock both of this parish were married by banns. Both signed. Witnesses were Cornelius Foot md John Woodmason

[Bigbury Parish Registers]

1759

Death of Arthur Shepard and Arthur Farewell - a gentleman

[Dorset County Records Office - Manorial Court Records Ref D45]

1759, 13th August

John Sullock and Mary Algar both of this parish were married by banns. John signed, Mary made her mark. Witnesses were Samuel Lambell and Cornelius Foot, both of whom signed.

1760-1801

Bigbury Mills and waste ground. (Woodmason, Taylor).

[D/MAP/T126 1760-1801 Dorset History Centre]

1760

4 leases

Easton

Pearce, Ilbert, Prettejohn

[1399M/3/3 1760 - 1860 Devon Record Office]

1760

Tenement and 4 acres of land called West Side the Path. (Adams, Legassicke).

[D/MAP/T134 1760-1811 Dorset History Centre]

1760

Bigbury Mills and waste ground. (Woodmason, Taylor).

[D/MAP/T126 1760-1801 Dorset History Centre]

1760

Boars Hill. (Cranch, Farwell, Dingle). Declaration of trust of Farwell's lease, 1793.

[D/MAP/T127 1760-1808 Dorset History Centre]

1761

Lease of premises called Burley Lake, South Huish - John Quarme, yeoman of South Huish to John Stidstone, husbandman of Bigbury.

[0922/1 7.01.1761 Cookworthy Museum]

1762

Closes called Efford South, and land called Tything Land (Harris), with appointment of attorney. (Prideaux).

[D/MAP/T128 1762 Dorset History Centre]

1763

Messuage and 8 acres. (Sullock)

[D/MAP/T129 1763 Dorset History Centre]

1763

Cottage and 2 perches of land. (Reeve).

[D/MAP/T130 1763 Dorset History Centre]

1764

Half a tenement, farthing of land (3½ acres) on Bigbury Down, and West Twelve Acres. (Knapman, Prideaux).

[D/MAP/T132 1764-1803 Dorset History Centre]

1764

Messuage, 8 acres of land and fields called Royal Hill and Baron Park. (Elliott, Hooppell).

[D/MAP/T133 1764,1816 Dorset History Centre]

1765

James Lane, Agnes his wife and James aged 7 yrs, Edward 5 yrs, Mary 3½ yrs, Ann 18 months, their children to Bigbury. Copy of the order.

[269A/PO 162 1765]

1766

Church Rate Assessment - Mary Sullock - 15 acres, 12s 6d for Coyte Park

[Bigbury History Society]

1767

Two cottages late Mary Barien's. (Lorne)

[D/MAP/T135 1767 Dorset History Centre]

1767

Thomas Brend, Ann his wife and William 20, Margery 13, Sarah 6, George 3½ and James 2½ from Bigbury (order for costs)

[1579A-0/24/45/23 1767 Devon Record Office]

1767

Lease and release John Hooppell of Bigbury, yeoman, to Richard Hamlyn of Bigbury, yeoman, in trust for John Hoopell.

[137M/T/5-6 1767 Devon Record Office]

1769

Third part of Bigbury Down called Outer Hext Down. (Square, Reeve).

[D/MAP/T136 1769-1806 Dorset History Centre]

c.1770

Draft examination of Eliz. Winn, servant to Jos. Elliot of W. Looe for 1 year 13 years ago, servant to Revd. Mr. Whitchair of Bigbury Devon for over 1 year, n.d.

[X155/596 (c.1770) Cornwall Record Office]

1770

Church Rate Assessment - Mary Sullock - 15 acres, 12s 6d for Coyte Park

[Bigbury History Society]

1774

Sarah Kerswell

Of Modbury, singlewoman, born there. Bound apprentice till twenty to Samuel Wakeham of Bigbury, cooper, with whom she served 5 yrs, then ran away, intent to complain to a justice of the peace, of the hard usage he made of her. On the road, her master overtook her, offered to cancel the indenture if she gave him 1s, to end all differences, which her mother paid; the indenture was cancelled. She settled in Bigbury, where it is hoped the parish will receive her, without giving Modbury the trouble of getting an order for her removal. (copy examination)

[269A/PO 49 1774 Devon Record Office]

1774

Smythson Tenement in Bigbury. (Goss, Dingle)

[D/MAP/T138 1774-1812 Dorset History Centre]

1774

Sarah Kerswell, singlewoman to Bigbury

[269A/PO 169 1774]

1777

William Basett

Born in the parish of Bigbury, bound parish apprentice to John White then of Bigbury, now of Plymouth. He lived there for 5 years or more. He removed with his master to Modbury and lived with him until he was about 18 yrs. Then his master gave him written permission to go where he pleased. He returned to Bigbury, lived with his father and took in cobbler's work and other work got for his own benefit til he was 21 yrs old. Then he went to Ringmore and worked with Thomas Wakeham, shoemaker for about 2½ yrs or more. When 24 yrs old the Ringmore parishoners grew uneasy at his living, he went to Bigbury, lived there for a week, returned to Modbury, lived there a 4-5 weeks, and master John White now lived at Modbury. He returned to Ringmore, lived in the same situation, for a year or two. Returned to Modbury, worked for different shoemakers, by the pair, lived there ever since. Never worked for John White or for his benefit, nor had any connections with him since his departure from him.

[269A/PO 54 1777 Devon Record Office]

1777, 17th November

Josias Sullock and Catherine Popplestone both of this parish were married by banns - both made marks

[Bigbury Parish Registers]

1776

Cottage and closes once George Hingston's. (Whiteare)

[D/MAP/T139 1776 Dorset History Centre]

1776

Cottage and land held by Mary Trinick. (Amm).

[D/MAP/T140 1776 Dorset History Centre]

1778

Moiety of tenement called Arthur Hills. (Elliott).

[D/MAP/T141 1778 Dorset History Centre]

1778

Moiety of messuage, 4 closes and 25 acres of land once Kitt's. (Elliott).

[D/MAP/T142 1778 Dorset History Centre]

1778

Four fields called New Parks, little meadow, barn and closes. (Elliott, Cole).

[D/MAP/T143 1778-1809 Dorset History Centre]

1779

Isaack Couch

Born in Aveton Gifford. When aged 7 yrs he was bound apprentice by private indenture to William Lee, late of Bigbury (since deceased) until aged 21 yrs. He served out his apprenticeship, lived with his master for two years at the end of his apprenticeship, as a hired servant by the year in Bigbury, remaining a bachelor. Never rented lands or tenements, nor executed any parish offices or paid parish rates or taxes. Lived with Mr Savory of Slade for 1 yr, and has since married. Now resides in Modbury with his wife, daughter Mary, who is over 30 yrs and unmarried, Honor, aged 29 yrs, unmarried, and that Honor has lived with the examinant since her birth.

[269A/PO 56 1779 Devon Record Office]

1780

John Ellis apprenticed to Richard Adams of Bigbury, yeoman

[269A/PO 785-786 1780]

1780

Church Rate Assessment – Mrs Sullock - l5 acres, £1 18s lOd for 2 Parals Park

[Bigbury History Society]

Peal of five bell hung in Bigbury Parish Church.

[Cookworthy Museum Village Notes]

21 June 1780

Will of Richard Adams, Yeoman of Bigbury , Devon

[Catalogue reference PROB 11/1066]

1781

Mortgage

1 John Ryder of Bigbury, yeoman

2 William Marshall of Kingsbridge, gent.

[1844/38 1781 Plymouth and West Devon Record Office]

1782

South part of Inner Hext Down. (Whiteare).

[D/MAP/T144 1782 Dorset History Centre]

1783 to 1794

George Sullock, curate of Parish Church

[Bigbury History Society]

1783

Messuage, 4 closes containing 8½ acres, and Loosewell Field. (Elliott).

[D/MAP/T145 1783 Dorset History Centre]

1784

John Haines

Sojourner of Bigbury. Believes he was born in Modbury, and lived with his father and mother until he was 7 yrs old, when his father went with him to Bigbury and put him to live with Thomas Pearce, gentleman, as an apprentice. His father told him to stay until he was aged 21 yrs, and then he was to have 3 suits of clothes. Does not know whether there was any indenture or not, but he never signed any indenture, to the best of his knowledge. He lived with Mr Pearce as agreed, received the clothes. Then he hired himself to Thomas Elliot of the same parish for 1 month on trial, which he served, then hired himself for 1 year at wages of 5 guineas, lived under it is hiring 7 months, when they disagreed and his master turned him off and paid his wages. Then he went to work by the week in the same parish for 2 masters for about 11 months. Then he married, and has three children, John, aged 30 yrs, now a mariner, James aged 29 yrs, who had gained a settlement in the parish, and his daughter aged 24 yrs 11 months who is now living with him.

[269A/PO 70 1784 Devon Record Office]

1785

Moiety of Tenement and 3 acres once Hugh Hingston's, and a field called Higher Cholborrow Down. (Elliott).

[D/MAP/T146 1785 Dorset History Centre]

1786

William Chipman

Born in Modbury, Aged 13-14 yrs was bound apprentice till aged 24 yrs to Robert Tope, at Penquit, Modbury. Lived there with him until aged 21 yrs old, when his master consented to his freedom, but would not give up his indenture until examinant was 24 yrs old. Left Robert Tope at the age of 21 yrs and went to live with his uncle Joseph Bickford, who kept a set of mills in Buckfastleigh, and another set in Staverton. He worked and lodged alternately in these parishes, but cannot say for how long. He worked for his uncle in this manner for 3-5 periods for 4-6 weeks each time, he could not remember. Between those times he returned and lodged sometimes at Mr Tope's in Modbury, sometimes at his mother's in same parish. Lived for a ½ yr with John Murphy at Keaton, Ermington and returned from thence to his uncle. Afterwards lived for 3/4 year with Mr Wooldridge of Modbury returned to his uncle, went to Modbury and married, which was before he was 24 yrs old. Went to Bigbury for a year in John Elliot's house, his brother in law, worked as a day-labourer. Returned to Modbury, where he lived ever since. Received no wages from his master, who knew his whereabouts, since aged 21 yrs. He cannot recall where he lived when he became 24 yrs old.

[269A/PO 90 1786 Devon Record Office]

1787

Millborough wood in Bigbury Manor. (Furlong)

[D/MAP/T147 1787 Dorset History Centre]

1787

Thomas Wakeham concerning William Bassett's settlement

Now of Ringmore, cordwainer. Apprenticed to John Whitell, cordwainer of Bigbury. William Bassett was also apprentice at the same time. John Whitell removed to Modbury, taking his apprentices with him. All lived there for 3-4 yrs. Then John Whitell dismissed William Bassett after a dispute, told him to work for his own advantage for any master, and was given a paper. Bassett lived with his father in Bigbury for 3-4 yrs, then agreed to work for Thomas Wakeham (who was then set up for himself in Bigbury) by the pair. Continued to work for ½ yr, when Wakeham removed to Kingswear, soon afterwards Bassett came there, worked & lodged in his house for ½ yr or more when Ringmore parish became uneasy.

Wakeham dismissed him from his employment 40 days before he was 24 yrs, thereupon he returned to Bigbury, then went to Modbury. Wakeham never made any agreement or conversation with John Whitell concerning Basett's working for a living with him, and constantly paid Bassett's wages.

[269A/PO 99 1787 Devon Record Office]

1789

Moiety of house and garden. (Reeve).

[D/MAP/T148 1789 Dorset History Centre]

1789

Tenement and three closes containing 6 acres. (Coker, Corker).

[D/MAP/T149 1789,1814 Dorset History Centre]

1792

Richard Stidston, sojourner in Newton Ferrers, born in Modbury, never apprenticed.

Hired as servant 15 yrs ago to Lewis Tucker of Halwell at £5. 5s. p.a. for 1 yr and £5. 15s for 1 yr, after lived with Uncle William White of Bigbury for 9 mths, then hired as servant to Mr Hines of Battisborough, Holbeton at £6. 6s p.a. but married after 6 mths and left after 1 mth more.

[2930A-2/PO 6/2 1792 Devon Record Office]

1792

Dwelling house and 3 acres, once Thomas Sullock's. (Couch).

[D/MAP/T150 1792 Dorset History Centre]

1793

Moiety of tenement, 6 acres of land and field called Dutch End Park. (Stidston, Elliott).

[D/MAP/T151 1793-1809 Dorset History Centre]

1793

Moiety of tenement and half a farthing of land. (Prideaux, Legassicke). Note concerning these two leases.

[D/MAP/T152 1793,1812 Dorset History Centre]

1793

Messuage and 90 acres (Farwell, Adams). Declaration of trust of lease, 1793. (Farwell).

[D/MAP/T137 1774-1794 Dorset History Centre]

1794

Cottage and ground where Randell Tenement once stood. (Hollett).

[D/MAP/T153 1794 Dorset History Centre]

1795

John BECK; Rank: Gunner; Born: Bigbury, Devon; Age on entry: 21; Dates served: 29 March 1795-23 September 1835

1796

Jonas Toms, 7 apprenticed to Nicholas Goss of Bigbury, gent

[269A/PO 998 1796]

1798, 3rd August

Marriage of William Sullock and Mary Skinner

[Bigbury Parish Register]

1798

Nilber camp 6th October 1798

This is to certify that William Sillock of the paish of Modbury, of the county of Devon was duly sworn and enrolled in the 4th Devon Regiment of Militia as a battolled man for the parish of Bigbury and the said William Sillock is now actually serving in the said regiment

(To the overseers of the poor of the parish of Bigbury) Hugh Pears Lt. Col.

[on reverse]

The said William Sillock requests the overseers of the parish of Bigbury to pay him fifty shillings parrish money conformable to Act of Parliament.

William Sillock appears in the 'majors company' of the regiment. He disappears after July 1799 with the note '22nd July attested to serve in the 4th regiment. Subsisted to 24 July'. This is 1799 not 1798.

[PW1 Mlitia Certificate, Exeter Records Office]

1801

4 acres of land called Lary Mill. (Joseph).

[D/MAP/T154 1801 Dorset History Centre]

1802

South west part of Randell's Cottage. (Hollett).

[D/MAP/T155 1802 Dorset History Centre]

11 November 1803

Abstract of Will of John Cuming, Yeoman of Bigbury, Devon

[Catalogue reference IR 26/342]

1804

Assignment to William Coad, to serve him during the residue of his apprenticeship, 1804

[Devon Record Office]

1804

List of offences committed by Robert Perraton and John Loverridge for an offence against the laws of Customs Also borough court examination of William Tickle, customs officer for the Port of Plymouth, who seized casks of rum and Geneva as well as a horse with all it's 'furniture', from Robert Perrittan of the parish of Bigbury

[1/695/10 1804 Plymouth and West Devon Record Office]

1804

Memorial window to Reverend J P Harris, who died at sea

Description Abstract of Will of Mary Cunning, Widow of Comeroy in Bigbury, Devon. Proved in the Court of Exeter.

Date January 06 1807

Catalogue reference IR 26/342

1806-1912

15 deeds and schedules. Easton and Braieswood

Goss, Pearce, Bird, Watts - Pitts

[1399M/3/2 1806 - 1912 Devon Record Office]

1806

Robert Treble from Bigbury

[5721 A/PO 199 1806]

January 02 1808

Abstract of Will of John Elliott, Yeoman of Bigbury, Devon. Proved in the Court of Exeter.

[Catalogue reference IR 26/343]

March 19 1808

Abstract of Will of Mary Ann Morgan, Widow of Bigbury, Devon. Proved in the Court of Exeter.

[Catalogue reference IR 26/343]

1809-1813

Licences to be absent from benefice

[2925 A/PI 1-2 1809 & 1813]

1809

Messuage, four closes, fields called Loosewell and Lower Cholborrow Down, 1809. (Elliott). Letter concerning this property, 1860.

[D/MAP/T156 1809,1860 Dorset History Centre]

November 05 1810

Abstract of Administration of John Sherrell, Yeoman of Bigbury, Devon. Proved in the Court of Exeter.

[Catalogue reference IR 26/343]

1812

Moiety of tenement and three acres of land, 1812. (Couch). Agreement concerning this property, 1857. (Farwell, Andrews). 10 letters, 1857, and income tax return, 1857.

[D/MAP/T157 1812,1857 Dorset History Centre]

1813

John Crocker of Bigbury, Devon

[1078/IRW/C/1430 1813 Devon Record Office]

1813

George Friend (9), apprenticed to Benjamin Hoopell of Bigbury, yeoman, no estate

[2930A-2/PO 20/12 1813]

1813, 20th November

George Sullock presented with the Office of Curate for Bigbury Parish on a stipend of £80 per year. He is to reside in the Parsonage House.

1814

Will - James Ryder of Bigbury, Devon

[1078/IRW/R/776 1814 Devon Record Office]

1820

John Cocker of Bigbury, Devon

[1078/IRW/C/745 1820 Devon Record Office]

25 November 1820

Description Will of John Lake, Blacksmith of Bigbury , Devon

[Catalogue reference PROB 11/1636]

1821

Johns, Elizabeth, age 11, apprenticed to Wroth, Samuel, yeoman, Bigbury Ugborough

[884/265/200 1821]

1822

Bigbury still vested in the heirs of the Duke of Bolton

[Lyson]

14 October 1823

Thomas SHORE; Rating; Age on entry: [Not Given]; Dates served: [Not Given]; Date and Type of Application: Whitehall 11 June 1861. For the additional following details Born: 14 October 1823, Plymouth, Devon,

[ADM 139/148 CS 14701]

1824

Mary Lang, alleged father William Randle of Bigbury Ugborough

[884/284/41 09/11/1824]

1824

Thomas Fox, Joan his wife, Jane aged 14 yrs, William aged 10 yrs, and Thomas Fox aged eight yrs, their children from Stoke Gabriel to Bigbury

[1981 A/PO 75 1824]

1824

Peter Morgan

Now residing in Aveton Giffard. Born in Bigbury, where his parents were legally settled. When he was 16 yrs old he bound himself apprentice to Walter Elliot of Stoke Gabriel, blacksmith. He is 38 yrs old next September. About 22 yrs ago, he bound himself, in 1802. The indenture was prepared by Mr Dawe of Totnes, schoolmaster. He was bound until aged 21 as a blacksmith, served out his time with Watler Elliot in Stoke Gabriel. He was then absent about nine or ten weeks, when he returned to the same master and hired himself for a year to the same master, for a year at five shillings a week. He lived there two years with Mr Eliot. Then he lived a quarter of a year, then he returned his father in Bigbury, remained there for 3 months. Then he lived for two months, in service, in Harberton. Then lived nine months in service, in Totnes, he married by banns in the parish church of Denbury, Elizabeth Shapley, by whom he has five children, Thomas 13, Mary Anne 10, Elizabeth 7, Anne 5, Peter 2. After he married, he lodged for 2 shillings a week at Plymouth, then for 3/6d a week, then 2s a week. Then he lived as a servant with Hancock at Knackers Hole. He rented a house and shop in North Huish. He rented rooms in Buckfastleigh for 1/6d a week. Then he lived for a few weeks in Chagford, then Newton Abbot, then Exeter, but never rented at £10 per year. Went to Aveton Gifford where he rents a shop for £2 per year and also occupies a leasehold tenement belonging to his father, worth two guineas a year. He has received relief several times from Stoke Gabriel, while living in Aveton

Giffard. Examination endorsed with a memorandum regarding his apprenticeship.

[2396A-1/PO 12 1824 Devon Record Office]

1829

Lease and release

1 David Roberts of Modbury, shopkeeper, and Lieutenant George Sullock of Highweek

2 Robert Hooppell of Bigbury, land surveyor

Waste Tor Down, part of Herroflood Estate

[567/85/1a and b 1829 Plymouth and West Devon Record Office]

1829

Warrant for apprehension of a lunatic

[2925 A/PC 1 1829]

20 March 1833

Description Name Foot, John Thomas

Place of Birth: Bigbury, Devon

Continuous Service Number: 32370

Date of Volunteering: 22 July 1856

Catalogue reference ADM 139/324

Dept Records of the Admiralty, Naval Forces, Royal Marines, Coastguard, and related bodies

Series Admiralty: Royal Navy Continuous Service Engagement Books

Piece 32301 - 32400

13 April 1833

Description Name Davis, Robert

Place of Birth: Bigbury, Devon

Continuous Service Number: 21075

Date of Volunteering: 23 October 1854

Catalogue reference ADM 139/211

Dept Records of the Admiralty, Naval Forces, Royal Marines, Coastguard, and related bodies

Series Admiralty: Royal Navy Continuous Service Engagement Books

Piece 21001 - 21100

22 May 1833

Ephraim SULLOCK; Rating; Age on entry: [Not Given]; Dates served: [Not Given]; Date and Type of Application: Whitehall 12 June 1861 and other. For the additional following details Born: 22 May 1833, Bigbury, Devon

[ADM 139/138 CS 13717]

24 August 1835

Description Name Barnens [Bardens], John

Place of Birth: Bigbury, Devon

Continuous Service Number: 27805

Date of Volunteering: 13 November 1855

Catalogue reference ADM 139/279

Dept Records of the Admiralty, Naval Forces, Royal Marines, Coastguard, and related bodies

Series Admiralty: Royal Navy Continuous Service Engagement Books

1836

Charity Woodmason of Bigbury, Devon

[1078/IRW/W/1220 1836 Devon Record Office]

1837

Amos Morgan of Foxhole, Bigbury, Devon

[1078/IRW/M/873 1837 Devon Record Office]

1838

William Dingle of Smithens, Bigbury, Devon

[1078/IRW/D/398 1838 Devon Record Office]

5 November 1840

Description Name Lang, Samuel

Official Number: 62994

Place of Birth: Bigbury, Devon

Catalogue reference ADM 188/43

Dept Records of the Admiralty, Naval Forces, Royal Marines, Coastguard, and related bodies

Series Admiralty: Royal Navy Registers of Seamen's Services

Piece 62801 - 63400

1840-1841

Bill of costs for the Houghton estate, Bigbury property of William Langmead

Philip Langmead owns Houghton Estate, having bought it from Gross

[81/FF/45 1840-1841 Plymouth and West Devon Record Office]

1841

Census

ADAMS, James, M, l5y, , Y, Haughton, 9100

ADAMS, Jane, F, 50y, , Y, Haughton, 9100

ADAMS, Joane, F, 20y, , Y, Haughton, 9100

ADAMS, Jobn, M, 20y, , Y, Haughton, 9100

ADAMS, John, M, 55y, Farmer, Y, Haughton, 9100

ADAMS, William, M, 25y, , Y, Haughton, 9100

ALLERY, Mary Ann, F, l0y, F S, Y, ??? Cumery, 9049

AMM, Elizabeth, F, 45y, , Y, St Anns Chapple, 9061

AMM, George, M 05y, , Y, St Anns Chapple, 9061

AMM, James, M, 45y, Tailor, Y, St Anns Chapple, 9061

AMM, Jane, F, 15y, , Y, St Anns Chapple, 9061

AMM, John, M, 10y, , Y, St Anns Chapple, 9061

AMM, Mary, F, 20y, , Y, St Anns Chapple, 9061

AMM, Simon, M, 09y, , Y, St Anns Chapple, 9061

AMM, Susan, F, 20y, , Y, St Anns Chapple, 9061

ANDREWS, John, M, 10y, , Y, Haughton, 9035

ANDREWS, John, M, 50y, Aglab, Y, Haughton, 9035

ANDREWS, susan, F, 50y, , Y, Haughton, 9035

BALPATCHETT, John, M, 65y, Pauper, Y, Sarlaborough Down, 91 03

BARDEN, Elizabeth, F, 08y, , Y, Village, 9027

BARDEN, John, M, 05y, , Y, Village, 9027

BARDEN, John, M, 35y, Shoemaker, Y, Village, 9027

BARDEN, Mary Ann, F, 40y, , Y, Village, 9027

BARDEN, Matilda, F, 03y, , Y, Village9027

BARDEN, Robert, M, 09y, , Y, Village, 9027

BARDEN, Stephen, M, 14y, , Y, Village, 9027

BARDENS, Elizabeth, F, 70y, Ind, Y, St Anns Chapple, 9063

BARDON, Eliza, F 11y, , Y, Bur Island, 9108

BARDON, Elizabeth, F, 14y, , Y, Bur Island, 9108

BARDON, Fanny, F, 40y, , Y, Bur Island, 9108

BARDON, Henry, M, 03y, , Y, Bur Island, 9108

BARDON, Jane, F, 20y, , Y, Bur Island, 9108

BARDON, John, M, 15y, , Y, Bur Island, 9108

BARDON, Joseph, M, 06y, , Y, Bur Island, 9108

BARDON, Maria, F, 12y, , Y, Bur Island, 9108

BARDON, Mary, F, 08y, , Y, Bur Island, 9108

BARDON, Simon, M, 10y, , Y, Bur Island, 9108

BARDON, Simon, M, 60y, Fisherman, Y, Bur Island, 9108

BARTLETT, George, M, 02y, , Y, Holwill, 9051

BARTLETT, Isaca, M, 06y, , Y, Holwill, 9051

BARTLETT, James, M, 40y, Ag lab, Y, Holwill, 9051

BARTIETT, Jane, F, 35y, , Y, Holwill, 9051

BARTLETT, William Sanders, M, 13y, , Y, Boars Hill, 9041

BASSETT, Ann, F, 20y, Svt, Y, ?? Combe Court, 9111

BASSETT, Eliza, F 10y, , Y, village, 9004

BASSETT, Elizabthe, F, 13y, , Y, Village, 9018

BASSETT, Hariot, F, 04y, , Y, Village, 9004

BASSETT, Henry, M, 15y, , Y, Village, 9018

BASSETT, James, M, 55y, Mason, Y, Village, 9018

BASSETT, John, M, 10y, , Y, Village, 9018

BASSETT, John, M, 45y, Ag lab, Y, Village, 9004

BASSETT, Joseph, M, 60y, Ag lab, Y, St Anns Chapple, 9058

BASSETT, Louisa, F, 08y, , Y, Village, 9018

BASSETT, Maria, F, 35y, , Y, Village, 9004

BASSETT, Mary, F, 50y, , Y, Village, 9018

BASSETT, Thomas, M, 30y, Mason, Y, ?? Combe Court, 9l 12

BASSETT, William, M, 01y, , Y, Village, 9004

BEA-LL, John, M, 13y, , Y, Village, 9025

BEARD, Mary, F, 60y, F S, Y, Easton, 9030

BEAVLE?, Jane, F, 11y, , Y, Holwell, 9045

BEAVLE?, Jane, F, 80y, Pauper, Y, Holwell, 9045

BEAVLE?, John, F, 45y, Ag lab, Y, Holwell, 9045

BEAVLE, Jane, F, 15y, , Y, St Anns Chappell, 9096

BEAVLE, Jane, F, 45y, , Y, St Anns Chappell, 9096

BEAVLE, Sisannah, F, 10y, , Y, St Anns Chappell, 9096

BEAVLE, William, M, 45y, Ag lab, Y, St Anns Chappell, 9096

BECK, Edward, M, 20y, , Y, Noddon, 9101

BECK, Jemima, F, 15y, , Y, Noddon, 9101

BECK, Mary, F, 60y, , Y, Noddon, 9101

BECK, Thomas, M, 70y, Farmer, Y, Noddon, 9101

BECK, William, M, 20y, , Y, Noddon, 9101

BEER, Agnes, F, 08y, , Y, Village, 9071

BEER, Ann, F, 45y, , Y, Anns Chaple, 9040

BEER, Ann, F, 75y, Pauper, Y, Village, 9007

BEER, Caterin, F, 01y, , Y, Village, 9071

BEER, Eleanor, F, 13y, Svt, Y, ?? Combe Court, 9111

BEER, George, M, 15y, Svt, Y, ?? Combe Court, 9111

BEER, Henry, M, 02y, , Y, Noddon, 9101

BEER, James, M, 05y, , Y, Village, 9003

BEER, Jane, F, 04y, , Y, Village 9003

BEER, Jane, F, 45y, , Y, Village, 9003

BEER, John, M, 02y, , Y, Foxhole, 9038

BEER, Jobn, M, 05y, , Y, Village, 9003

BEER, John, M, 40y, Ag lab, Y, Village, 9071

BEER, Joseph, M, 05y, , Y, Village, 9077

BEER, Mary Ann, F, 15y, , Y, ?? Coombe Cottage, 9060

BEER, Mary, F, 25y, Pauper, Y, Foxhole, 9038

BEER, Nicholas, M, 05y, , Y, Village, 9003

BEER, Susan, F, 40y, , Y, Village, 9071

BEER, Susanna, F, 04y, , Y, Village, 9071

BEER, William, M, 06y, , Y, Foxhole, 9038

BEER, William, M, 07y, , Y, Village, 9072

BEER, William, M, 35y, Ag lab, Y, Village, 9003

BEER, William, M 50y, An lab, Y, Ann Chaple, 9040

BICKHAM, Aron, M, 04y, , Y, Village, 9080

BICKHAM, Mary Ann, F, 02y, , Y, Village, 9080

BOON, Joanna, F, 70y, Pauper, Y, Village, 9010

BREND?, James, M, 75y, Pauper, Y, Village, 9069

BREND?, Mary, F, 85?, Pauper, Y, Village, 9069

BREND, George, M, 04y, , Y, Milbro Cott, 9114

BREND, Jane, F, 05y, , Y, Village, 9002

BREND, Mary Ann, F, 01y, , Y, Village, 9002

BREND, Mary Jane, F, 02y, , Y, Milbro Cott, 9114

BREND, Mary, F, 30y, , Y, Milbro Cott, 9114

BREND, Richard, M, 10y, y, Y, Village, 9002

BREND, Samuel, M, 12y, Svt, Y, Haughton, 9100

BREND, Samuel, M, 25y, Ag lab, Y, Milbro Cott, 9114

BREND, Sarah, M, 05y, , Y, Village, 9002

BREND, Sarah, F, 35y, , Y, Village, 9002

BREND, Thomas, M, 06y, , Y, Milbro Cott, 9114

BREND, William, M, 08y, , Y, Milbro Cott, 9114

BREND, William, M, 40y, Ag lab,Y, Village, 9002

BROWN, Ann, F, 40y, , Y, Village, 9084

BROWN, Elizabeth, F, l3y, , Y, Village, 9084

BROWN, John, M, l5y, Pauper, Y, Village, 9084

BROWN, John, M, 40y, Ag lab, Y, Village, 9084

BROWN, Louisa, F, 11y, , Y, Village, 9084

BROWN, Mary Ann, F, l5Y, , Y, Village, 9084

BROWN, Philip, M, 15y, Svt, Y, Easton, 9030

BROWN, Richard, M, 05y, , Y, Village, 9084

BROWN, William, M, 07Y, , Y, Village, 9084

BURLEY, Ann, F, l5y, , Y, Dukesmill, 9036

BURLEY, George, M, 15y, Svt, Y, ??? Cumery, 9049

BURLEY, James, M, 45y, Ag lab, Y, Dukesmill, 9036

BURLEY, Rachel, F, 12y, , Y, Dukesmill, 9036

BURLEY, Susan, F, 45y, , Y, Dukesmill, 9036

COCKER, Alice, F, 10y, , Y, Village, 9014

COCKER, Alice, F, 35y, , Y, Village, 9014

COCKER, Ann Cole, F, 09m, , , Y, St Anns Chapple, 9063

COCKER, Deborah, F, 02y, , Y, St Anns Chapple, 9063

COCKER, Eliza, F, 12y, , Y, St Anns Chapple, 9063

COCKER, Emley, F, 06y, , Y, St Ann Chapple, 9063

COCKER, George, M, 01y, , Y, Village, 9029

COCKER, Grace, F, 03y, , Y, Village, 9029

COCKER, Jane Bardens, F, 14y, F S, Y, ??? Cumery, 9048

COCKER, Jane, F, 10y, , Y, Village, 9029

COCKER, Jane, F, 37y, , Y, Village, 9029

COCKER, Jane, F, 40y, , Y, St Anns Chapple, 9063

COCKER, Jane, F, 65y, , Y, Village, 9014

COCKER, John, M 04y, , Y, St Anns Chapple, 9063

COCKER, John, M, 15y, , Y, Village, 9029

COCKER, John, M, 40y, , Y, St Anns Chapple, 9063

COCKER, Judith, F, 05y, , Y, Village, 9029

COCKER, Mary Cole, F, 12y, , Y, Village, 9029

COCKER, Owen Cole, M, l0y, , Y, Village, 9029

COCKER, Philip, M, 08y, , Y, Village, 9029

COCKER, Philip, M, 40y, Farmer, Y, Village, 9029

COCKER, Philip, M, 70y, Carpenter, Y, Village, 9029

COCKER, Wilmot Ford, F, 08y, , Y, St Anns Chapple,9063

COLE, Ann, F, 50y, , Y, Village, 9001

COLE, George, M, 60y, Farmer, Y, Village, 9001

COUCH, Elizabeth, F, 50y, Svt, Y, Knowle, 9047

COUCH, Eunice, F, 07y, , Y, Village, 9083

COUCH, Robert, M, l0y, , Y, Hexdown, 9110

COUCH, Sarah, F, 35y, , Y, Village, 9083

CROUCH, Elizabeth, F, l5y, Ap, Y, Holwill, 9056

CROUCH, George, M, 13y, M S, Y, Holwill, 9056

CUMING, Elizabeth, F, 02y, , Y, Dukesrnill, 9037

CUMING, Elizabeth, F, 30y, , Y, ??? Cunery, 9049

CUMING, Elizabeth, F, 35y, , Y, Dukesmill, 9037

CUMING, Garland, M, 05m, , Y, ??? Cumery, 9049

CUMING, Hannah, F, 30y, , Y, ??? Cumery, 9048

CUMING, John, M, 04y, , Y, Dukesmill, 9037

CUMING, John, M, 25y, Farmer, Y, ??? Curnery, 9049

CUMING, Mary, F, 06y, , Y, Dukesmill, 9037

CUMING, Pamela, F, 08y, , Y, Dukesmill, 9037

CUMING, Richard, M, 30y, Farmer, Y, ??? Cumery, 9048

CUMING, Richmd, M, 35y, Miller, Y, Dukesmill, 9037

CUMING, Walter John, M, 01y, ,Y, ??? Cumery, 9049

DAVIS, Eliza, F, 11y, ap, Y, Village, 9094

DAVIS, Samuel, M, 10y, ap lab, Y, Noddon, 9101

DAW, Sarah, F, 65y, , Y, Hingston, 9116

DINGLE, Elizabeth, F, 50y, Ind, Y, West Smithons, 9046

DINGLE, Joseph, M, l5y, , Y, West Smithons, 9046

DOLTON, Samuel, M, 65y, Ag lab, Y, Village, 9088

DOLTON, Sarah, F, 65y, , Y, Village, 9088

DOLTON, Susan, F, l5y, Ap, Y, Holwill, 9056

EDWARDS, Ann, F, 11y, , Y, Sedgewill Cottages, 9109

EDWARDS, Eliza, F, 03y, , Y, Sedgewill Cottages, 9l09

EDWARDS, Elizabeth, F, o7y, , Y, Sedgewill Cottages, 9109

EDWARDS, John, M, 25y, Ag lab, Y, Sedgewill Cottages, 9109

EDWARDS, Mary, F, 30y, , Y, Sedgewill Cottages, 9109

EDWARDS, Robert, M, 40y, Ag lab, Y, Sedgewill Cottages, 9109

EDWARDS, William, M, l5y, , Y, Sedgewill Cottages, 9109

ELLIS, Ann, F, 30y, Svt, Y, ?? Folly, 9118

ELLIS, Jane, F, o3y, , Y, Village, 9015

ELLIS, Jane, F, 30y, , Y, Village, 9015

ELLIS, Owen Cocker, M, o5y, , Y, Village, 9015

ELLIS, Susm Sarah, F, oly, , Y, Village, 9015

ELLIS, William, M, 35y, Millwright, Y, Village, 90l5

ELWORTHY, Georgianna, F, 25y, Svt, Y, ?? Combe Court, 9111

FARLY, Ann, F, 10y, , Y, Village, 9007

FARLY, Elizabeth, F, l5y, Svt, Y, Village, 9117

FARLY, Elizabeth, F, 65y, Pauper, Y, Village, 9003

FARLY, Emma, F, o7y, , Y, Village, 9007

FARLY, James, M, o5y, , Y, Village, 9007

FARLY, John, M, loy, , Y, Village, 9007

FARLY, Philip, M, 45y, Ag lab, Y, Village, 9007

FARLY, Sally, F, 40y, , Y, Village, 9007

FLETCHER?, Pricilla, F, 30y, Svt, Y, Halwell Coombe, 9039

FOALE, George, M, 30y, Ag lab, Y, Village, 9029

FOALE, John Widdon, M, o3y, , Y, Warren, 9105

FOALE, John Widdon, M, 55y, Smith, Y, St Anns Chapple, 9062

FOALE, John, M, 30y, Smith, Y, St Anns Chapple, 9062

FOALE, Joseph Talbut, M, oly, , Y, Warren, 9105

FOALE, Margaret, F, 40y, , Y, St Anns Chapple, 9062

FOALE, Maria, F, 25y, , Y, Warren, 9105

FOALE, Mary, F, 05m, , Y, St Anns Chapple, 9062

FOOT, Eliza, F, loy, , Y, Village, 9003

FOOT, John, M, o8y, , Y, Village, 9095

FOOT, Joseph, M, 14y, Svt, Y, Village, 9089

FOOT, Richard, M, 40y, Tailor, Y, Village, 9095

FOOT, William, M, 15y, , Y, Village, 9095

FORD, Luisa Tayler, F, 13y, , Y, Boars Hill, 9041

FOX, Jane, F, 60y, , Y, Village, 9092

FOX, Thomas, M, 25y, ,Y, Village, 9092

FOX, Thomas, M, 60y, Ag lab, Y, Village, 9092

FOX, William, M, 30y, , Y, Village, 9092

FREEMAN, Elizabeth, F, 55y, , Y, Hingston, 9116

FRIEND, Edward, M, 25y, , Y, Hexdown Cottage, 9121

FRIEND, Eliza, F, 11y, , Y, Foxhole, 9033

FRIEND, Elizabeth, F, 04y, , Y, Foxhole, 9033

FRIEND, George, M, 30y, Svt, Y, Parsonage House, 9031

FRIEND, Jemima, F, 30y, , Y, Foxhole, 9033

FRIEND, Lavinia A, F, 03w, , Y, Hexdown Cottage, 9121

FRIEND, Mary Ann Eliza, F, 0ly, , Y, Hoxdown Cottage, 9121

FRIEND, Mary Ann, F, 25y, , Y, Hexdown Cottage, 9121

FRIEND, Sarah Ann, F, 07Y, , Y, Foxhole, 9033

FROST, James, M, l5y, AP, Y, Bayles, 9044

FROUDE, William, M, 15y, Svt, Y, Village, 9070

FULL, Mary, F, 25y, Svt, Y, Halwell Coombe, 9039

FURZEMAN, James, M, 45y, Schoolmaster, Y, Village, 9013

FURZEMAN, Jane, F, 50y, , Y, Village, 9013

GARD, Elizabeth, F, 20y, , Y, Hingston, 9116

GERMAN, Joseph, M, 13y, Svt, Y, Village, 9073

GILL, Nicholas, M, 55y, Farmer, Y, Knowle, 9047

GILLARD, Elizabeth, F, 65y, Pauper, Y, Village, 9098

GIST, Elizabeth, F, 35y, , Y, ??Coombe Cottage, 9060

GIST, John, M, 40y, Ag lab, Y, ?? Coombe Cottage, 9060

GOODMAN, Elizabeth, F, 03y, , Y, St Anns Chapple, 9057

GOODMAN, Francis, M, 14y, Ap lab, Y, Hingston, 9116

GOODMAN, James, M, 12y, , Y, St Anns Chapple, 9057

GOODMAN, Jemima, F, 05y, , Y, St Anns Chapple, 9057

GOODMAN, John, M, 40y, Ag lab, Y, St Anns Chapple, 9057

GOODMAN, Maria, F, 35y, , Y, St Anns Chapple, 9057

GOODMAN, Philip, M, 10y, , Y, St Anns Chapple, 9057

HAMBLYN, Jemima, F, 11y, F S, Y, Hexdown Cottage, 9121

HAMLYN, Elizabeth, F, 10y, , Y, Lincombe ? Cottage, 9119

HAMLYN, Infant male, M, 04d, , Y, Lincombe ? Cottage, 9l 19

HAMLYN, John, M, 09m, Y, Hexdown, 9110

HAMLYN, Thomas, M, 03y, , Y, Lincombe ? Cottage, 119

HAMLYN, Thomas, M, 30y, Ag lab, Y, Lincombe ? Cottage, 9119

HAMM, Thomas, M, 55y, Army pens, Y, Village, 9086

HARDY, Eleanor, F, 09y, , Y, Village, 9016

HARDY, George, M, 03Y, , Y, Village, 9016

HARDY, Mary Ann, F, 03m, , Y, Village, 9016

HARDY, Mary, F, 30y, , Y, Village, 9016

HARDY, William, M, 30y, Mariner, Y, Village, 9016

HILL, Sarah, F, 60y, , Y, Village, 9028

HILL, William, M, 60y, Ag lab, Y, Village, 9028

HINGSTON, Andrew, M, 07y, , Y, Bayles, 9044

HINGSTON, Andrew, M, 30y, Farmer, Y, Bayles, 9044

HINGSTON, Elizabeth, F, 15y, Svt, Y, Village, 9094

HINGSTON, Elizabeth, F, 70y, , Y, Village, 9024

HINGSTON, George, M, 70y, Ag lab, Y, Village, 9024

HINGSTON, Grace, F, 50y, , Y, Village, 9120

HINGSTON, Honor, F, 05y, , Y, Bayles, 9044

HINGSTON, John, M 01y, , Y, Bayles, 9044

HINGSTON, John, M, 40y, Ag lab, Y, Village, 9120

HINGSTON, Mary Ann, F, 30y, , Y, Bayles, 9044

HINGSTON, Mary, F, 03y, , Y, Bayles, 9044

HINGSTON, Philip, M, 20y, Svt, Y, Village, 9001

HINGSTON, William, M, l3y, Svt, Y, ??? Cumery, 9048

HOBLETT, Edwin, M, 20y, , Y, Village, 9073

HOBLETT, Elizabeth, F, 90y, Ind, Y, Village, 9107

HOBLETT, Jane, F, 55y, Ind, Y, Village, 9107

HOBLETT, Sarah, F, 35y, Ind farmer, Y, Village, 9073

HODGE, Mary, F, 75y, Pauper, Y, Holwill, 9052

HODGE, Thomas, M, 15y, Svt, Y, Haughton, 9100

HOOPELL, Samuel, M, 03y, , Y, Holwill, 9052

HOOPELL, Samuel, M, 30y, Ag lab, Y, Holwill, 9052

HOOPELL, Susan, F, 40Y, , Y, Holwill, 9052

HOOPELL, William, M, 05y, , Y, Holwill, 9052

HOOPPELL, Benjamin, M, 30y, Farmer, Y, Hexdown, 9110

HOOPPELL, Benjamin, M, 65y, Farrner, Y, Village, 9094

HOOPPELL, Dinah, F, 25y, , Y, Hexdown, 9110

HOOPPELL, Grace, F, 35y, , Y, Holwill, 9056

HOOPPELL, Joan, F, 60y, , Y, Village, 9094

HOOPPELL, John, M, 09Y, , Y, Holwill, 9056

HOOPPELL, Maria, F, 0ly, , Y, Holwill, 9056

HOOPPELL. Mary Grace, F, 04y, , Y, Holwill, 9056

HOOPPELL, Robert, M, 11y, , Y, Holwill, 9056

HOOPPELL, Robert, M, 20y, Svt, Y, Village, 9094

HOOPPELL, William, M, l3y, , Y, Holwill, 9056

HOOPPELL, William, M, 50y, Farmer, Y, Holwill, 9056

HORSWILL, Elizabeth, F, 08y, , Y, Holwell, 9045

HORSWILL, Elizabeth, F, 75y, , Y, Village, 9098

HORSWILL, Grace, F, 40y, , Y, Village, 9019

HORSWILL, John, M, 15y, Ap, Y, Easton, 9030

HORSWILL, John, M, 70y, Ag lab, Y, Village, 9098

HORSWILL, William, M, 13y, Ap, Y, Village, 9094

HUXTABLE, William, M, 30y, Ag lab, Y, Village, 9029

JEFFERY, Benjamin, M, l5y, Svt, Y, Knowle, 9047

KITT, Eleanor, F, l5Y, , Y, Vi[age, 902l

KITT, Mary, F, 60y, , Y, Village, 9021

KITT, Nicholas, M, 30y, Svt, Y, ??? Cumery, 9048

KITT, Thomas, M, 6Oy, Ag lab, Y, Village, 9021

KITT, William, M, l5y, Svt, Y, ??? Cumery, 9049

LANE, Edward, M, 11y, Y, Hexdown, 9110

LANE, Elizabeth, F, l5y, Svt, Y, Village, 9001

LANE, James, M, 11y, , Y, Village, 9087

LANE, James, M, 50y, Shoemaker, Y, Vilage, 9087

LANE, John, M, 25y, Ag lab, Y, Sarlaborough Down, 9104

LANE, Joseph, M, 15y, M S, Y, Easton, 9030

LANE, Susan, F, 13y, , Y, Village, 9087

LANE, Susan, F, 40y, , Y, Village, 9087

LANE, William, M, 20y, Shoemaker, Y, Hexdown, 9110

LAPTHORN, Jane, F, 35y, , Y, Village, 9013

LAPTHORN, Mary Jane, F, 09y, , Y, Village, 9013

LAWRENCE ?, Augustus G, M, 40y, Farmer, N, Halwell Coombe, 9039

LAWRENCE ?, Henrietta Louisa, F, 50y, , N, Halwell Coombe, 9039

LAWRENCE ?, Julia ? Louisa, F, 75y, Ind, N, Halwell Coombe, 9039

LEAR, Catherine, F, 25y, , Y, Village, 9064

LEAR, Catherine, F, 55y, , Y, Village, 9064

LEAR, John, M, 55y, Tallow chandler, Y, Village, 9064

LEGASSICK, Esther, F, 10y, , Y, Village, 9071

LEGASSICK, Jane, F, 30y, , Y, Village, 9026

LEGASSICK, Richard, M, 60y, Mason, Y, Village, 9071

LEGASSICK, Susan, F, 65y, Pauper, Y, Village, 907l

LEGASSICK, William, M, 02y, , Y, Village, 9026

LEGASSICK, William, M, 30y, Mason, Y, Village, 9026

LEIGH, Edwin, M, 02w, , Y, Village, 9006

LEIGH, Jonathan, M, 07y, , Y, Village, 9006

LEIGH, Rebecca, F, 25y, , Y, Village, 9006

LEIGH, Rmma, F, 04y, , Y, Village, 9006

LEIGE, Robert, M, 25y, Ag lab, Y, Village, 9006

LEIGH, Sarah, F, 70y, Pauper, Y, Village, 9014

LEIGH, Thomas, M, 0ly, , Y, Village, 9006

LEVY ? Francis Daniel, M, 50y, Lieut RN, N, Halwell Coombe 9039

LUCKCRAFT, John, M, 0lm, , Y, ?? Combe Court, 9113

LUCKCRAFT, May, F, 25y, , Y, ?? Combe Court, 9113

LUCKCRAFT, Thomas, M 25y, Smith, Y, ?? Combe Court, 9113

LUSCOMBE, Henry, M, 50y, Farmer, Y, Boars Hill, 9041

LUSCOMBE, Lucy, F, 50y, , Y, Boars Hill, 9041

LYNDON, Jane, F, 20y, , Y, Sarlaborough Down, 9104

LYNDON, Mary Jane, F, 06m, , Y, Sarlaborough Down, 9104

LYNDON, Philip, M, 25y, Ag lab, Y, Salaborough Down, 9104

MEADOWS, Jane, F, l5y, , Y, Village, 9081

MEADOWS, John, M, 45y, Ag lab, Y, Village, 9081

MEADOWS, Mary Ann, F, l3y, , Y, Village, 9081

MEADOWS, Priscilla, F, 55y, , Y, Village, 9081

MILDON, Edward, M, 05m, , Y, Village, 9020

MILDON, Elizabeth Horswill, F, 14y, , Y, Village, 9020

MILDON, Elizabeth, F, 40y, , Y, Village, 9020

MILDON, Grace, F, 03y, , Y, Village, 9020

MILDON, James, M, l5Y, Ap, Y, Village, 9094

MILDON, James, M, 45y, Ag lab, Y, Village, 9020

MILDON, John Horswill, M, l0y, , Y, Village, 9020

MILDON, Mary Horswill, F, 05y, , Y, Village, 9020

MILDON, Thomas, M, l2y, , Y, Village, 9020

MILDON, William, M, 07y, , Y, Village, 9098

MILLER, Elizabeth, F, 35y, , Y, Village, 9072

MILLER, Jane, F, O7y, , Y, Village, 9072

MILLER, John, M, 10y, Svt, Y, ?? Combe Court, 9111

MILLER, John, M, 4Oy, Ag lab, Y, Village, 9072

MILLER, Margaret, F, 06y, , Y, Village, 9072

MILLER, Thomas, M, l4y, Ap lab, Y, Holwill, 9O56

MILLER, William, M, 04Y, , Y, Village, 9072

MITCHELMORE, Elizabeth, F, 15y, Ap, Y, Haughton, 9100

MITCHELMORE, Walter, M, l2y, Ap lab,Y, Hingston, 9116

MOORE, Fanny, F, 12y, , Y, Shoulder Furze, 9043

MOORE, Harry, M, 60y, Shepherd, Y, Shoulder Furze, 9043

MORGAN, Alice Jane, F, l4y, , Y, Foxhole, 9032

MORGAN, Amos, M, l5y, , Y, Foxhole, 9032

MORGAN, Mary Ann, F, O2y, , Y, Foxhole, 9032

MORGAN, Peter, M, 07y, , Y, Foxhole, 9032

MORGAN, Susan, F, 4Oy, , Y, Foxhole, 9032

MORGAN, Thomas, M, 5Oy, Farmer, Y, Foxhole, 9032

MOYAN, James, M, l5y, Ap lab,Y, Holwill, 9056

PARRATON, George, M, 2Oy, Svt, Y, Village, 9089

PARRATON, Henry, M, 35y, , Y, Village, 9070

PARRATON, Richard, M, 12y, Svt, Y, Village, 9070

PARRATON, Robert, M, 75y, Farmer, Y, Village, 9O7O

PEARCE, Thomas, M, 5Oy, Farmer, Y, Easton, 9030

PENGILLY, James, M, o6y, , Y, Village, 9012

PENGILLY, Susan, F, 25y, , Y, Village, 9012

PENGILLY, Thomas, M, oly, , Y, Village, 9012

PENGILLY, Thomas, M, 25y, Ag lab, Y, Village, 9012

PENGILLY, William, M, o5y, , Y, Village, 9012

PENJILLY, Elizabeth, F, lOy, Pauper, Y, Village, 9090

PENJILLY, Mary, F, 75y, Pauper, Y, Village, 9084

PEPPERELL, James, M, 35y, Farmer, Y, Village, 9106

PEPPERELL, Sofia, F, 3Oy, , Y, Village, 9106

PEPPERELL, Thomas, M, 11y, , Y, Village, 9106

PEPPERELL, William, M, o7y, , Y, Village, 9106

PERRATON, Jobn, M, 4Oy, Ag lab, Y, Village, 9028

PERRETT, William, M, 3oy, Ag lab, Y, St Anns Chapple, 9059

PHILIPS, Mary Ann, F, 11y, , Y, Village, 9092

PITTS, May, F, oly, , Y, Village, 9085

PITTS, Samuel, M, 3oy, Ag lab, Y, Village, 9085

PITTS, Susan, F, 25y, ,Y, Village, 9085

POUND, Ann, F, 35y, , Y, Village, 9097

POUND, George, M, 35y, Ag lab, Y, Village, 9097

POUND, Jobn, M, o5y, , Y, Village, 9097

POUND, Mary Parraton, F, 1oy, , Y, Village, 9097

POUND, Sarah Ann, F, oly, , Y, Village, 9097

POWELL, Ann, F, 14y, , N, Village, 909l

POWELL, George, M, o6y, , I, Village, 9091

POWELL, Mary, F, o5y, , I, Village, 909l

POWELL, Mary, F, 35y, , Y, Village, 909l

POWELL, Susan, F, 10y, , I, Village, 9091

POWELL, William, M, 02y, , Y, Village, 909l

POWELL, William, M, 45y, Army pens, N, Village, 9091

PRICE, Elizabeth, F, 3Oy, Svy, Y, Parsonage House, 9031

PROWSE, Elizabeth, F, 7Oy, Pauper, Y, Village, 9072

PULLYBLANK, John, M, 20y, Ag lab, Y, Village, 9022

PULLYBLANK, John, M, 5Oy, Ag lab, Y, Village, 9022

PULLYBLANK, Martha, F, 6Oy, , Y, Village, 9O22

PULLYBLANK, Robert, M, 2Oy, Ag lab, Y, Village, 9022

REEVE, Amelia Jane, F, Oly, , Y, ?? FollY, 9118

REEVE, Amelia, F, 25y, , Y, ?? FollY, 9118

REEVE, Ann, F, l5y, , Y, Village, 9066

REEVE, Catherine, F, 06y, , Y, Village, 9118

REEVE, Edwrad, M, 04y, , Y, Village, 9078

REEVE, Eliza, F, 12y, Svt, Y, Haughton, 9100

REEVE, Elizabeth, F,09y, , Y, Village, 9078

REEVE, James, M, 30y, Farmer, Y, ?? Folly, 9118

REEVE, John, M, 30y, Fisherman, Y, Village, 9066

REEVE, Jobn, M, 45y, Ag lab, Y, Village, 9082

REEVE, Mary Ann, F, 11y, , Y, Village, 9078

REEVE, Mary, F, O4y, , Y, ?? FollY, 9l18

REEVE, Mary, F, 7oy, Pauper, Y, Village, 9066

REEVE, Sarah, F, 02y, , Y, Village, 9078

REEVE, Sarah, F, 35y, , Y, Village, 9078

REEVE, Thomas, M, 4Oy, Ag lab, Y, Village, 9078

REEVE, William, M, l5y, , Y, Village,9066

REEVE, William, M, 35y, Farmer, Y, Village, 9065

RENDLE, Ann' F, o8Y, , Y, Holwill, 9054

RENDLE, Ann, F, 5Oy,, Y, Holwill, 9055

RENDLE, Christopher, M, 65y, Ag lab, Y, Holwill, 9055

RENDLE, Elizabeth, F, 25y, , Y, Holwill, 9055

RENDLE, George, M, o5y, , Y, Holwill, 9054

RENDLE, George, M, l5y, Ap lab, Y, Holwill, 9056

RENDLE, Jane, F, 35y, , Y, Holwill, 9054

RENDLE, John, M, o3y, , Y, Holwill, 9054

RENDLE, John, M, 25y, Ag lab, Y, Holwill, 9054

RENDLE, Louisa, F, l5y, , Y, ?? Combe Court, 9112

RENDLE, Marcia, F, 3Oy, , Y, Holwill, 9055

RENDLE, Mary Anm, F, 35y, , Y, ?? Combe Court, 9112

RENDLE, Robert, M, 2Oy, Ag lab, Y, Hohrill, 9055

RENDLE, Thomas, M, 2oy, Ag lab, Y, Holwill, 9055

RENDLE, William, M, 35y, Ag lab, Y, ?? Combe Court, 9ll2

ROACH, Ann, F, 11y, , Y, Shoulder Furze, 9042

ROACH, Ann, F, 55y, , Y, Village, 9017

ROACH, Christopher, M, 11y, , Y, Village, 9023

ROACH, Christopher, M, 4Oy, Ag lab, Y, Shoulder Furze, 9042

ROACH, George, M, o4y, , Y, Shoulder Ftmze,X)42

ROACH, George, M, l3y, , Y, Village, 9023

ROACH, Grace, F, l5y, , Y, Shoulder Furze, 9042

ROACH, James, M, o6y, , Y, Shoulder Furze, 9042

ROACH, Jobn, M, 55y, Ag lab, Y, Village, 9017

ROACH, Mary, F, l2y, F S, Y, West Smithons, 9046

ROACH, Nicholas, M, o6y, , Y, Village, 9023

ROACH, Nicholas, M, 4Oy, Ag lab, Y, Village, 9023

ROACH, Susanna, F, 35y, , Y, Shoulder Furze, 9042

ROACH, William, M, o2y, , Y, Shoulder Furze, 9042

RYDER, Catherine, F, 2Oy, Svt, Y, Village, 9070

SANDERS, Charles, M, o1y, , Y, Village, 9l17

SANDERS, Edwin, M, 14Y, , Y, Village, 9117

SANDERS, Frederick, M, 12y, , Y, Village, 9117

SANDERS, Henry, M, o6y, , Y, Village, 9117

SANDERS, John, M, 40y, Publican, Y, Village, 9117

SANDERS, Mary Jane, F, o3y, , Y, Village, 9117

SANDERS, Mary, F, 40y, , Y, Village, 9117

SANDERS, Thomas, M, 30y, Thatcher, Y, Holwill, 9051

SANDERS, William, M, l5y, , Y, Village, 9117

SHEPHERD, James, M, 25y, Ag lab, Y, Holwill, 9053

SHEPHERD, James, M, 45y, Ag lab, Y, Holwill, 9053

SHEPHERD, John, M, 2Oy, Ag lab, Y, Holwill, 9053

SHEPHERD, Mary, F, 55y, , Y, Holwill, 9053

SKINNER, Ann, F, 6Oy, , Y, Village, 9050

SKINNER, Jobn, M, 35y, Ag lab, Y, Village, 9011

SKINNER, John, M, 8Oy, Ag lab, Y, Village, 9050

SKINNER, Samuel, M, oly, , Y, Village, 9011

SKINNER, Sarah, F, o8y, , Y, Village, 9011

SKINNER, Sarah, F, 3Oy, , Y, Village, 9011

SKINNER, Thomas, M, 65y, Pauper, Y, Village, 9081

SKINNER, William, M, o3y, , Y, Village, 9oll

STEER, Caroline, F, o9y, , Y, Village, 9019

STEER, Elizabeth, F, o8y, , Y, Village, 9074

STEER, Elizabeth, F, 25y, , Y, Village, 9070

STEER, Elizabeth, F, 3Oy, , Y, Village, 9074

STEER, Fanny, F, 75y, Pauper, Y, Village, 9023

STEER, Francis, M, 2oy, Shoemaker, Y, ?? Combe Court, 9112

STEER, Francis, M, 5Oy, Carpenter, Y, Village, 9oO8

STEER, Frederick, M, 12y, , Y, Village, 9019

STEER, Hannah Mary, F, o7y, , Y, Village, 9019

STEER, James, M, o6y, , Y, Village, 9O74

STEER, Jane, F, O9y, , Y, Village, 9065

STEER, John, M, 4oy, Thatcher, Y, Village, 9019

STEER, Kitty, F, 4Oy, , Y, Village, 9019

STEER, Margaret, F, O2y, , Y, Village, 9074

STEER, Mary Ann, F, l5y, , Y, Village, 9076

STEER, Mary Grace, F, lom, , Y, Village, 9070

STEER, Mary, F, 45y, ,Y, Village, 9065

STEER, Mary, F, 5Oy, ,Y, Village, 9oo8

STEER, Robert, M, 25y, Ag lab, Y, Village, 9081

STEER, Robert, M, 50y, Ag lab, Y, Village, 9076

STEER, Sarah An, F, O2y, , Y, Village, 9019

STEER, Simon, M, 25y, Carpenter, Y, Village, 9070

STEER, Susan, F, 1ly, , Y, Village, 9065

STEER, Susan, F, 25y, , Y, Village, 9081

STEER, Susanna Elizabeth, F, O2y, , Y, Village, 9070

STEER, Thomas jnr, M, 20y, , Y, Village, 9065

STEER, Thomas, M, 45y, Carpenter, Y, Village, 9065

STEER, Triphena, F, 2Oy, Pauper, Y, Village, 9076

STEER, William, M, 35y, Hawker, Y, Village, 9074

TALBUT, John, M, 55y, Ag lab, Y, Warren, 9105

TALBUT, Mary Ann, F, 25y, , Y, Warren, 9105

TALBUT, Susan, F, 50y, , Y, Warren, 9105

TAYLER, Catherine, F, l5y, F S, Y, Village, 9094

TAYLOR, Catherine, F, o3y, , Y, Noddon Mill, 9102

TAYLOR, Catherine, F, l5y, , Y, Village, 9067

TAYLOR, Edward, M, O7y, , Y, Noddon Mill, 9l02

TAYLOR, Gilbert, M, l5y, , Y, Village, 9067

TAYLOR, James,M, 35y, Miller, Y, Noddon Mill, 9102

TAYLOR, Jemima, F, O5y, , Y, Noddon Mill, 9102

TAYLOR, Jemima, F, o7y, , Y, Village, 9067

TAYLOR, Joanna, F, 30y, , Y, Noddon Mill, 9102

TAYLOR, Kezia, F, O2y, , Y, Village, 9067

TAYLOR, Martin, M, o3m, , Y, Village, 9067

TAYLOR, Martin, M, 4Oy, Farmer, Y, Village, 9067

TAYLOR, Mary Jane, F, o5y, , Y, Village, 9067

TAYLOR, Rhoda, F, O7y, , Y, Village, 9067

TAYLOR, Rhoda, F, 35y, , Y, Village, 9067

TAYLOR, Sarah, F, 11y, , Y, Hexdown, 9ll0

TERREY, George, M, l5y, M S, Y, Holwill, 9056

TERRY, Eliza, F, l5y, , Y, Village, 9075

TERRY, Elizabeth, F, l5y, , Y, Village, 9O99

TERRY, George, M 4oy, Mason, Y, Village, 9099

TERRY, Hariot, F, l2y, , Y, Village, 9070

TERRY, Henry, M, lOy, , Y, Village, 9089

TERRY, James, M, loy, , Svt, Y, Village, 9001

TERRY, Jane, F, 7Oy, , Y, Village, 9089

TERRY, Joanna, F, 4Oy, , Y, Village, 9099

TERRY, John Edward, M, 07y, , Y, Village, 9075

TERRY, John, M, 05y, , Y, Village, 9099

TERRY, John, M, 55y, Farmer, Y, Village, 9075

TERRY, Maria, F, 3Oy, , Y, Village, 9089

TERRY, Mary, F, 50y, , Y, Village, 9075

TERRY, Richard, M, 35y, , Y, Village, 9089

TERRY, Richard, M, 75y, Mason, Y, Village, 9089

TERRY, Robert, M, O8y, , Y, Village, 9099

TERRY, Sally, F, l5y, F S, Y, Easton, 9030

TERRY, Susan, F, 10y, , Y, Village, 9099

TERRY, Walter, M, 02y, , Y, Village, 9099

TERRY, William, M, 12y, , Y, Village, 9099

TIDDY, Ann, F, 20y, Ind, Y, Village, 9001

TIPPETT, William, M, 25y, Ag lab, Y, Village, 9009

TOMS, Ann, F, 60y, , Y, Village, 9079

TOMS, Elizabeth, F, 11y, , Y, Village, 9077

TOMS, Elizabeth, F, 25y, , Y, Village, 9O77

TOMS, Elizabeth, F, 35y, , Y, Village, 9005

TOMS, Hariett, F, O1y, , Y, Village, 9005

TOMS, Jobn, M, o8y, , Y, Village, 9077

TOMS, John, M, 35y, Ag lab, Y, Village, 9005

TOMS, Mary Ann, F, 04y, , Y, Village, 9077

TOMS, Mary Jane, F, 03y, , Y, Village, 9005

TOMS, Mary, F, 15y, , Y, Village, 9079

TOMS, Rebecca, F, 2Oy, , Y, Sarlaborough Down, 9103

TOMS, Richard, M, l5y, Ap lab, Y, ?? Folly, 9118

TOMS, Robert, M, 2Oy, Ag lab, Y, Sarlaborough Down, 9103

TOMS, Samuel, M, o1y, , Y, Village, 9090

TOMS, Sarah, F, 25y, Pauper, Y, Village, 9090

TOMS, Susan, F, 04m, , Y, Village, 9077

TOMS, Thomas, M, Oly, , Y, Sarlaborough Down, 9103

TOMS, William, M, 04y, , Y, Village, 9090

TOMS, William, M, 35y, Ag lab, Y, Village, 9077

TOMS, William, M, 6Oy, Ag lab, Y, Village, 9079

TRANT, Charlotte, F, 2oy, , Y, Hingston, 9l16

TRANT, Mary, F, 6oy, , Y, Hingston, 9l16

TRANT, Myra, F, o5y, , Y, Hingston,9l16

TRANT, Philip, M, 3oy, , Y, Hingson, 9l16

TRANT, Sarah, F, O2y, , Y, Hingston, 9l16

TRANT, Sarah F, 25y, , Y, Hingston, 9l16

TRIGGS, Catherine, F, lOy, , Y, Village, 9025

TRIGGS, Jobn, M, 7oy, Pedlar, Y, Village, 9025

TRUTE, Thomas, M, 35y, M S, Y, Halwell Coombe, 9039

TUCKER, Robert, M, l5y, Svt, Y, ?? Combe Court, 9111

VOISEY, Ellza, F, o3y, , Y, Foxhole, 9038

VOISEY, Elizabeth, F, l5y, F S, Y, Bayles, 9O44

VOISEY, Mary, F, 5Oy, Pauper, Y, Foxhole 9038

VOISEY, William, M, 2Oy, Svt, Y, Dukesmill, 9037

WARD, William, M, 25y, Svt, Y, Hingston, 9116

WARDEN, Ann, F, 6oy, , Y, ??? Cumery, 9049

WARDEN, Jobn, M, 6Oy, Ind, Y, ??? Cumery, 9049

WEBB, Ann, F, 35y, , Y, Village, 9010

WEBB, George, M, o7y, , Y, Village, 9Olo

WEBB, John, M, l3y, , Y, Village, 9010

WEBB, Thomas, M, o3y, , Y, Village, 9010

WEBB, William, M, o9y, , Y, Village, 9Olo

WHAKEHAM, Emma, F , O2y, , Y, Milbro Cott, 9115

WHAKEHAM, George, M, o4y, , Y, Milbro Cott, 9115

WHAKEHAM, Henry, M, o8y, , Y, Milbro Cott, 9115

WHAKEHAM, James, M, o6y, , Y, Milbro Cott, 9115

WHAKEHAM, James, M, l2y, M S, Y, Village, 9075

WHAKEHAM, John, M, l3y, , Y, Milbro Cott, 9115

WHAKEHAM, John, M, 20y, Svt, Y, Village, 9073

WHAKEHAM, Maria, F, 35y, , Y, Milbro Cott, 9115

WHAKEHAM, Nicholas, M, 35y, Ag lab, Y, Milbro Cott, 9115

WHAKEAM, Sarah, F, 65y, Pauper, Y, Village, 9095

WHAKHAM, Betsy, F, 08y, , Y, Village, 9009

WHAKHAM, Chartity, F, 45y, , Y, Village, 9080

WHAKHAM, Elizabeth, F, 11y, , Y, Village, 9080

WHAKHAM, Grace, F, 40y, , Y, Village, 9009

WHAKHAM, Jane, F, 15y, , Y, Village, 9068

WHAKHAM, Jane, F, l5y, , Y, Village, 9080

WHAKHAM, John, M, 04y, , Y, Village, 9009

WHAKHAM, Nicholas, M, l5y, , Y, Village, 9080

WHAKHAM, Polley, F, 45y, , Y, Village, 9068

WHAKHAM, Richard, M, 06y, , Y, Village, 9009

WHAKHAM, Richard, M, 40y, Ag lab, Y, Village, 9009

WHAKHAM, Samuel, M, l2y, , Y, Village, 9080

WHAKHAM, Samuel, M, 45y, Ag lab, Y, Village, 9068

WHAKHAM, William, M, 10y, , Y, Village, 9068

WHAKHAM, William, M, 50y, Pauper, Y, Village, 9080

WILTON, Agnes, F, 60y, , Y, Village, 9086

WILTON, Aron, M, 25y, Ag lab, Y, Village, 9086

WILTON, Henry, M, l5y, , Y, Village, 9086

WILTON, Janes, M, 60y, Tailor, Y, Village, 9086

WILTON, John, M, 45y, Ag lab, Y, Tussland ?, 9093

WILTON, Mary, F, 55y, ,Y, Tussland ?, 9093

WILTON, Richard, M, 20y, J Carpenter, Y, St Anns Chapple,9062

WINSLAND, Phebe, F, l4y, Svt, Y, Village, 9073

WINTER, John, M, 20y, Farmer, Y, Knowle, 9047

WOODMASON, Amelia, F, 06y, , Y, Dukesmill, 9034

WOODMASON, Eleanor, F, 25y, , Y, Dukesmill, 9034

WOODMASON, Irene Jemima, F, 04y, , Y, Dukesmill, 9034

WOODMASON, John, M, 25y, Svt, Y, West Smithons, 9046

WOODMASON, William, M, loy, Svt, Y, West Smithons, 9046

WOODMASON, William, M, 25y, Road mender?, Y, Dukesmill, 9034

WROTH, Charles, M, O7y, , Y, ?? Combe Court, 9111

WROTH, Edward, M, 03y, , Y, ?? Combe Court, 9111

WROTH, Jane Hodder, F, loy, , Y, ?? Combe Court, 9111

WROTH, John, M, l5y, , Y, ?? Combe Court, 9111

WROTH, Mary Hodder, F, 05y, , Y, ?? Combe Court, 911l

WROTH, Mary, F, 4Oy, , Y, ?? Combe Court, 9111

WROTH, Samuel, M, 25y, , Y, ?? Combe Court, 9111

WROTH, Samuel, M, 50y, Yeoman, Y, ?? Combe Court, 9111

WROTH, Servington Hodder, M, ,20y, Malster, Y, ?? Combe Court, 9111

WROTH, Walter, M, l5y, Mariner, Y, ?? Combe Court, 9111

WROTH, William, M, 15y, , Y, ?? Combe Court, 9111

18 January 1842

Release of Portions charged on Higher and Lower Costley Meadows, Filham Moor and hereditaments in the Parish of Ugborough under a Settlement made on the Marriage of William Rivers with Elizabeth Morris both now deceased.

(1)Samuel Wroth of Bigbury, exor. of Samuel Wroth decd. late of Modbury, Maltster, trustee under the settlement.

(2)William Rivers of Ivy Bridge, Innkeeper. William Howell of Exeter, Steam Packet Agent and Eliza his wife, she and William Rivers being the surviving children of the late William and Elizabeth Rivers.

(3)Richard Derry of Plymouth, Esq.

Recites the Marriage Settlement of 1801. Elizabeth Rivers has lately died, a widow. William and Eliza are now entitled to £1,200 which Richard Derry is willing to pay on the release and surrender of the term of 200 years of the trusteeship. Samuel Wroth now surrenders the remainder of the term of 200 years held on Costley Meadows and Filham Moor.

Signed/sealed Samuel Wroth William Rivers William Howell Eliza Howell

[1392/8 18 January 1842 Plymouth and West Devon Record Office]

1843

The Duke of Cleveland is now Lord of the Manor. Duke owns Court Barton Estate - Samual Wroth occupies.

[Tithe Returns]

Walter Prettejohn owns Houghton Estate - John Adams occupies

Duke of Cleveland owns Tuffland Farm - Samual Wroth leased – Samual Wroth Junior occupies

Brockington owns Noddon Farm - Thomas Beck occupies

Nicholas Gill owns and occupies Knowles Tenement [Farm] & E[ast?] Smitham Tenement

Elizabeth Dingle occupies W[est?] Smithan [as written] from the Duke of Cleveland

Terence Livingtone – Rector

Duke of Cleveland's Tenants:

Elizabeth Hingston leased – Samual Wroth Occupied – Pit Tenement & 2 houses

Robert Hooppell Leased – Thomas Fox Occupied – Millborough Tenement. Hooppell retained some Fields

Robert Hooppell leased 5 houses with fields, gardens, and or orchards – Robert Parraton occupied

Benjamin Hooppell leased and occupied 2 houses & fields

George Cole leased and occupied 1 house, a garden and an orchard

Elizabeth Hingston leased – George Cole occupied – 2 houses, gardens and fields

Richard Cole leased – Nicholas Roach occupied – Willings Tenement – House, garden orchard and fields

Martin Taylor leased and occupied Tullocks[? Perhaps Sullock's] tenement

Philip Crocker leased and occupied Looms & Creese Tenement

Richard Tarry leased and occupied a house, garden and fields

George Tarry leased and occupied a house and garden

Thomas Steer leased and occupied a house and garden

William Hooppell leased – William Reeve occupied a house and garden

Thomas Luckraft leased and occupied a house and garden

John Reeve leased – William Hamm Occupied – a house and garden

Edward Howlett leased and occupied Rendle's Tenement

John Saunders leased and occupied Upper Cottage Tenement including 2 houses

William Hooppell leased – William Steer occupied a house and garden

William Hooppell leased – Samual Wills occupied a house and garden

William Hooppell leased – John Tarry occupied a house, garden and fields

Edwn Hollett leased – Agnes Wilton occupied a house and garden

John Reeve leased – George Pound occupied a house

1844

Release

1 Robert Stephens Jago of Plymouth, esq

2 Thomas Bewes of Plymouth, esq

Manor of Houghton, Bigbury

[81/FF/47 1844 Plymouth and West Devon Record Office]

1844

Schedule of title deeds of the Manor of Houghton, Bigbury

[81/FF/46 1844 Plymouth and West Devon Record Office]

24 July 1845

Description Name Toms, Albert

Official Number: 46823

Place of Birth: Bigbury, Devon

Catalogue reference ADM 188/16

Dept Records of the Admiralty, Naval Forces, Royal Marines, Coastguard, and related bodies

Series Admiralty: Royal Navy Registers of Seamen's Services

Piece 46601 - 47200

1846

Will - Richard Terry of Bigbury, Devon

[1078/IRW/T/221 1846 Devon Record Office]

1846

Will - Philip Trant of Bigbury, Devon

[1078/IRW/T/558 1846 Devon Record Office]

1847

Copyhold admission to moiety of customary tenement called Lower Conroy (75a)

[149/1 4 August 1847 Plymouth and West Devon Record Office]

1847

Pilchard fishing was a huge industry for the people of the South Hams. In one instance during the early nineteenth century a haul of Pilchards worth around £7,000 was taken in one year.

'... the bulk of the fish [Pilchards] passes between Scilly and Land's End, and entering the English Channel, follows the windings of the shore as far as Bigbury Bay'

[Penzance Natural History and Antiquarian Society]

31 December 1849

Description Name Skinner, Henry

Official Number: 46514

Place of Birth: Bigbury, Devon

Dept Records of the Admiralty, Naval Forces, Royal Marines, Coastguard, and related bodies

Series Admiralty: Royal Navy Registers of Seamen's Services

Piece 46001 - 46600

[Catalogue reference ADM 188/15]

1850

Duke of Cleveland & Countess Dowager of Sandwich Lords of Manor, but part of the manor belongs to W L Prettejohn and other smaller owners.

Poor of the Paish are left 'an interest of 25' [pounds?] by Mr Lee and Mr Lowe

Robert Harry Fortescue – Curate of Bigbury Parish Church

Philip Cocker – Victualler of the Royal Oak Inn

William Andrews - Farmer, Houghton Estate

Richard Cuming - Farmer, Cumery

Samual Wroth - Farmer, Tuffland

Richard Foot -Taylor

Jane Hallett – Shopkeeper

James Woodmason, Thomas Luckraft – Basketmaker

John Bardens, John Coaker, John Lane – Shoemakers

Simon Steer, Thomas Steer, Thomas Steer junior – Carpenters

Nicholas Roach, John Terry – Carriers

Richard Crocker, John Cumming, Nicholas Gill, William Gill, James Grant, John Hancock, Andrew Hingston, Benjamin Hooppell, Amos Morgan, Harry Parraton, Thomas Pearse, James Pepperell, William Pepperell, William Reeve, Richard Terry – Farmers

[Cookworthy Museum Village Notes]

1851

The names, and number of people of that name, from Census.

The location of the records are available through DFHS Publication '1851 Census Surname Index – Number 13'

Adams (1)	Amm (2)	Andrews (3)	

Bardens (2)	Beer (5)	Bartlett (2)	Bictford (1)
Basset (1)	Boon (2)	Beard (1)	Brend (4)
Baker (1)	Beavell (2)	Brown (3)	
Ball (1)	Beck (1)	Burley (2)	

Cocker (2)	Codd (1)	Cole (1)	Colliver (1)
Couch (4)	Cowles (1)	Crocker (1)	Cuming (1)
Cumming (1)	Curson (1)		

Dingle (1)	Dolton (1)

Evans (1)

Farley (2)	Foale (3)	Foot (2)	Ford (2)
Fotescue (1)	Fox (1)	Freerman (2)	Friend (1)

Gill (1)	Garland (1)	Gillard (1)	Gilley (2)
Goodman (3)	Grant (1)		

Hamlye (1)	Hamlyn (1)	Hamon (1)	Hancock (1)

Hanover (1)　　Hardey (1)　　Harding (1)　　Hart (1)
Harvey (2)　　Hill (1)　　　Hines (1)　　　Hingston (4)
Hollett (2)　　Hooppell (5)　　Horswell (1)　　Horswill (3)
Hutchuns (1)

Jeffery (1)

Kitt (2)

Lear (2)　　　Luckraft (1)　　Light (1)　　Lister (1)
Lavers (1)　　Luscombe (1)　　Lane (2)　　Leigh (3)

Meadows (1)　　Mildon (3)　　Miller (4)　　Mitchelmore (1)
Mitchmore (1)　　Moore (1)　　Morgan (1)

Naryulion (1)

Pollyblank (1)　　Parraton (1)　　Parrot (2)　　Partridge (2)
Pearce (1)　　　Pengilley (2)　　Pengilly (1)　　Pepprell (2)
Perry (1)　　　Perreton (1)　　Pound (1)　　Powell (2)
Pitts (1)　　　Prowse (1)　　　Purdy (1)

Randel (1)　　Rendle (1)　　Randle (4)　　Rider (1)
Roach (5)　　Ryder (4)　　Reeve (5)

Sanders (3)　　Symons (1)　　Shepherd (1)　　Sherriff (1)
Skinner (2)　　Steer (6)

Talbut (1)　　Taylor (5)　　Terrey (3)　　Toms (4)
Triggs (2)
Voisey (1)

Ward (3)   Wroth (3)   Warden (1)   Weymouth (1)
Woodmason (1) Wilton (1)   Wakeham (5)

1851

Edward Foot of Bigbury, Devon

[1078/IRW/F/219 1851 Devon Record Office]

1851

Will - Richard Terrey of Bigbury, Devon

[1078/IRW/T/222 1851 Devon Record Office]

1852

Valuation of Bigbury Court.

[D/MAP/E55 1852 Dorset History Centre]

13 January 1853

Description Name Brown, Philip

Official Number: 61639

Place of Birth: Bigbury, Devon

Dept Records of the Admiralty, Naval Forces, Royal Marines, Coastguard, and related bodies

Series Admiralty: Royal Navy Registers of Seamen's Services

Piece 61601 - 62200

[Catalogue reference ADM 188/41]

1853

Will - George Cole of Bigbury, Devon

[1078/IRW/C/812 1853 Devon Record Office]

1853

John Triggs of Bigbury, Devon

[1078/IRW/T/659 1853 Devon Record Office]

1854

Robert Hooppell of Bigbury, Devon

[1078/IRW/H/1302 1854 Devon Record Office]

1854

Philip Cocker of Bigbury, Devon

[1078/IRW/C/746 1854 Devon Record Office]

1854

Richard Ford of Bigbury, Devon

[1078/IRW/F/276 1854 Devon Record Office]

1856

Robert Perraton of Bigbury, Devon

[1078/IRW/P/630 1856 Devon Record Office]

1856

Mary Beard of Bigbury, Devon

[1078/IRW/B/540 1856 Devon Record Office]

26 May 1856

Description Name Bear, John William

Official Number: 106052

Place of Birth: Bigbury Kingsbridge, Devon

Dept Records of the Admiralty, Naval Forces, Royal Marines, Coastguard, and related bodies

Series Admiralty: Royal Navy Registers of Seamen's Services

Piece 106001 - 106500

[Catalogue reference ADM 188/127]

27 November 1856

Description Name Wakeham, James

Official Number: 105640

Place of Birth: Bigbury Kingsbridge, Devon

Dept Records of the Admiralty, Naval Forces, Royal Marines, Coastguard, and related bodies

Series Admiralty: Royal Navy Registers of Seamen's Services

Piece 105501 - 106000

[Catalogue reference ADM 188/126]

1856

Samual Wroth, farmer, occupies Court Barton Estate.

[Cookworthy Musaun Village Notes]

1857

Infant School [built?]. Supported by Minister. There are 15 to 20 children, with Sarah Pound as Mistress.

14 July 1857

Description Name Beer, Thomas

Official Number: 105605

Place of Birth: Bigbury Kingsbridge, Devon

Dept Records of the Admiralty, Naval Forces, Royal Marines, Coastguard, and related bodies

Series Admiralty: Royal Navy Registers of Seamen's Services

Piece 105501 - 106000

[Catalogue reference ADM 188/126]

11 December 1857

Description Name Wilton, John William

Official Number: 105662

Place of Birth: Bigbury Modbury, Devon

Dept Records of the Admiralty, Naval Forces, Royal Marines, Coastguard, and related bodies

Series Admiralty: Royal Navy Registers of Seamen's Services

Piece 105501 - 106000

[Catalogue reference ADM 188/126]

1857

M Gueritz - Curate of Bigbury Parish Church

G Terry – Clerk

Samual Wroth, farmer and maltster, occupies Court Barton Estate

Philip Cocker - Victualler of the Royal Oak Inn and a farmer

Richard Andrew - Farmer, Houghton Estate

Mary Beck – Farmer, Noddon Farm

James Adams - Farmer, Lower Cumery

Robert Hooppell - Farmer, High Cumery

Samual Wroth junior - Farmer, Tufflad & Higher Shearlangstone

William Gill - Farmer, Knowle Farm

Mrs Nancy Cole, John Bardens – Shoemaker and shopkeeper

John Crocker - Shoemaker

Joseph Dingle – Farmer at West Smithens

John Hancock - Farmer and carrier

Mary and Harry Hingston - Farmers

Edward Hollett - Farmer at Rendles

Jane Hollett - Shopkeeper

Benjamin Hooppell - farmer at Willings

Thomas Luckraft - Blacksmith

Harry Parraton - Farmer

Nicholas Roach – Shopkeeper and carrier

Thomas Saunders - Thatcher

Francis Steer - Carpenter

John Steer- Thatcher

Simon Steer - Carpenter

Thomas Steer senior - Carpenter

Thomas Steer junior - Wheelwright

John Terry - Shopkeeper

Nicholas Wakeham - Marine Stores

William Woodmason – Basketmaker

[Cookworthy Museum Village Notes]

01 May 1858

Description Name Wakeham, John

Official Number: 106046

Place of Birth: Bigbury Kingsbridge, Devon

Dept Records of the Admiralty, Naval Forces, Royal Marines, Coastguard, and related bodies

Series Admiralty: Royal Navy Registers of Seamen's Services

Piece 106001 - 106500

[Catalogue reference ADM 188/127]

17 November 1858

Description Name Saunders, William John

Official Number: 91519

Place of Birth: Bigbury, Devon

Dept Records of the Admiralty, Naval Forces, Royal Marines, Coastguard, and related bodies

Series Admiralty: Royal Navy Registers of Seamen's Services

Piece 91401 - 92000

[Catalogue reference ADM 188/99]

03 May 1860

Description Name Treeby, Samuel

Official Number: 91824

Place of Birth: Bigbury, Devon

Dept Records of the Admiralty, Naval Forces, Royal Marines, Coastguard, and related bodies

Series Admiralty: Royal Navy Registers of Seamen's Services

Piece 91401 - 92000

[Catalogue reference ADM 188/99]

08 April 1860

Description Name Hooppell, Samuel John

Official Number: 91245

Place of Birth: Bigbury, Devon

Dept Records of the Admiralty, Naval Forces, Royal Marines, Coastguard, and related bodies

Series Admiralty: Royal Navy Registers of Seamen's Services

Piece 90801 - 91400

[Catalogue reference ADM 188/98]

14 January 1864

Description Name Lugger, William Walter

Official Number: 113055

Place of Birth: Bigbury, Devon

Dept Records of the Admiralty, Naval Forces, Royal Marines, Coastguard, and related bodies

Series Admiralty: Royal Navy Registers of Seamen's Services

Piece 113001 - 113500

[Catalogue reference ADM 188/141]

16 June 1864

Description Name Widger, John Thomas

Official Number: 126388

Place of Birth: Bigbury, Devon

Dept Records of the Admiralty, Naval Forces, Royal Marines, Coastguard, and related bodies

Series Admiralty: Royal Navy Registers of Seamen's Services

Piece 126001 - 126500

[Catalogue reference ADM 188/167]

04 January 1865

Description Name Davis, Thomas

Official Number: 115874

Place of Birth: Bigbury, Devon

Dept Records of the Admiralty, Naval Forces, Royal Marines, Coastguard, and related bodies

Series Admiralty: Royal Navy Registers of Seamen's Services

Piece 115501 - 116000

[Catalogue reference ADM 188/146]

27 March 1865

Description Name Brown, James Reeves

Official Number: 113133

Place of Birth: Bigbury, Devon

Dept Records of the Admiralty, Naval Forces, Royal Marines, Coastguard, and related bodies

Series Admiralty: Royal Navy Registers of Seamen's Services

Piece 113001 - 113500

[Catalogue reference ADM 188/141]

1866

Baptist Chapel Built in village

[Cookworthy Museum Village Notes]

20 January 1866

Date of Volunteering

Name Toms, Albert

Place of Birth: Bigbury, Devon

[Continuous Service Number: 38475A]

1866, 29th August

Marriage of John Sullock and Jane Crocker – Residence listed as 'Dameral's Combe, Aveton Gifford, Bigbury'

1866

Poor rate assessment for Bigbury, DEVON.

[D/MAP/E173 1866 Dorset History Centre]

1867

Draft valuation of manor of Bigbury, and lands in the parishes of Aveton Gifford and Plymouth.

[D/MAP/E56 1867 Dorset History Centre]

1867

Letters concerning lands in Towednack, and in manor of Pendrim, CORNWALL: estates at Bigbury, E. Portlemouth, Plymouth and Woolston, DEVON.

[D/MAP/E180 1867 Dorset History Centre]

1867

Schedule of lands in the manors of Bigbury, Woolston and East Portlemouth.

[D/MAP/E96 1867 Dorset History Centre]

1867

Schedule of leaseholds in the manor and parish of Bigbury

[D/MAP/E97 1867 Dorset History Centre]

28 February 1867

Description Name Bunker, William Robert

Official Number: 121298

Place of Birth: Bigbury, Devon

Dept Records of the Admiralty, Naval Forces, Royal Marines, Coastguard, and related bodies

Series Admiralty: Royal Navy Registers of Seamen's Services

Piece 121001 - 121500

[Catalogue reference ADM 188/157]

1867-1883

Papers concerning Devon estates including plans of Aveton Gifford, 1867, and Brixham, N.D.; reference and tithe reference to the Brixham plan, 1867, schedule of heath lands in Brixham, N.D.; abstract summary of Devon estates in Bigbury, Brixham, E. Portlemouth and Woolston, 1868; notes on Devon rents, 1867; references to lands in Aveton Gifford, Bigbury, East Portlemouth and Woolston, 1867; letters and copy bill for valuation of additional lands in Little Hempston.

[D/MAP/E186 1867-1883 Dorset History Centre]

1868

Valuation of manor of Bigbury, and lands in the parishes of Aveton Gifford and Plymouth, with plan.

[D/MAP/E57 1868 Dorset History Centre]

1868 April 9

John LUSCOMBE of Combe Royal, West Alvington, co. Devon and Samuel WROTH of Bigbury, co. Devon to Emma Ann CHURCHILL.of Wood Estate, Woodleigh, co. Devon

[DEV 3/7/254 1868 April 9 Museum of English Rural Life]

12 April 1869

Description Name Goodman, George

Official Number: 133261

Place of Birth: Bigbury, Devon

Dept Records of the Admiralty, Naval Forces, Royal Marines, Coastguard, and related bodies

Series Admiralty: Royal Navy Registers of Seamen's Services

Piece 133001 - 133500

[Catalogue reference ADM 188/181]

19 October 1869

Description Name Brown, William Henry

Official Number: 134615

Place of Birth: Bigbury, Devon

Dept Records of the Admiralty, Naval Forces, Royal Marines, Coastguard, and related bodies

Series Admiralty: Royal Navy Registers of Seamen's Services

Piece 134501 - 135000

[Catalogue reference ADM 188/184]

07 February 1870

Description Name Bardens, William Simon

Official Number: 147254

Place of Birth: Bigbury, Devon

Dept Records of the Admiralty, Naval Forces, Royal Marines, Coastguard, and related bodies

Series Admiralty: Royal Navy Registers of Seamen's Services

Piece 147001 - 147500

[Catalogue reference ADM 188/209]

26 February 1870

Description Name Goodman, Edward

Official Number: 136191

Place of Birth: Bigbury, Devon

Dept Records of the Admiralty, Naval Forces, Royal Marines, Coastguard, and related bodies

Series Admiralty: Royal Navy Registers of Seamen's Services

Piece 136001 - 136500

[Catalogue reference ADM 188/187]

10 October 1870

Description Name Ryder, John Henry

Official Number: 147511

Place of Birth: Bigbury, Devon

Dept Records of the Admiralty, Naval Forces, Royal Marines, Coastguard, and related bodies

Series Admiralty: Royal Navy Registers of Seamen's Services

Piece 147501 - 148000

[Catalogue reference ADM 188/210]

06 August 1871

Description Name Bunker, John

Official Number: 143536

Place of Birth: Bigbury near Kingsbridge, Devon

Dept Records of the Admiralty, Naval Forces, Royal Marines, Coastguard, and related bodies

Series Admiralty: Royal Navy Registers of Seamen's Services

Piece 143501 - 144000

[Catalogue reference ADM 188/202]

17 September 1871

Description Name Rendle, Samuel Francis

Official Number: 158298

Place of Birth: Bigbury, Devon

Dept Records of the Admiralty, Naval Forces, Royal Marines, Coastguard, and related bodies

Series Admiralty: Royal Navy Registers of Seamen's Services

Piece 158001 - 158500

[Catalogue reference ADM 188/231]

1871

Board School built for 120 children

[Cookworthy Museum Village Notes]

09 June 1872

Description Name Goodman, Harry

Official Number: 144234

Place of Birth: Bigbury, Devon

Dept Records of the Admiralty, Naval Forces, Royal Marines, Coastguard, and related bodies

Series Admiralty: Royal Navy Registers of Seamen's Services

Piece 144001 - 144500

[Catalogue reference ADM 188/203]

1872

Fire in St Lawrence Church. Church is rebuilt and restored following lightning strike.

[Cookworthy Museum Village Notes]

08 December 1873

Description Name Goodman, William John

Official Number: 280942

Place of Birth: Bigbury, Devon

Dept Records of the Admiralty, Naval Forces, Royal Marines, Coastguard, and related bodies

Series Admiralty: Royal Navy Registers of Seamen's Services

Piece 280501-281000

[Catalogue reference ADM 188/448]

16 November 1873

Description Name Lane, Tom

Official Number: 148229

Place of Birth: Bigbury, Devon

Dept Records of the Admiralty, Naval Forces, Royal Marines, Coastguard, and related bodies

Series Admiralty: Royal Navy Registers of Seamen's Services

Piece 148001 - 148500

[Catalogue reference ADM 188/211]

20 March 1874

Description Name Barnes, Philip John

Official Number: 153997

Place of Birth: Bigbury, Devon

Dept Records of the Admiralty, Naval Forces, Royal Marines, Coastguard, and related bodies

Series Admiralty: Royal Navy Registers of Seamen's Services

Piece 153501 - 154000

[Catalogue reference ADM 188/222]

1875

Joseph Foot - occupier of the Royal Oak Inn

William Wroth - Farmer, Tuffland

J Pepperell - Farmer, Frogland

A Hannaford - Farmer, Knowle Farm

Reverend Farrer - Rector

John Hancock – Carrier & farmer

Harry Perraton - Farmer

Nicholas Roach – Shopkeeper & carrier

Thomas Steer - Wheelwright

Simon Steer - Carpenter

Jsnes Wakeham – F rmer, Willings

[Cookworthy Museum Village Notes]

1877

Lease for 14 years

1. Andrew Foss of Buckfastleigh, yeoman, Richard Jackson of Diptford, yeoman, Rev. William Cooper Johnson of Diptford clerk, Thomas Butland of Diptford gent., Peter Richard Foss, George Furneaux Samuel Jackson, Edmund Parnell Jackson, all of Diptford, yeoman, William Furneaux of Buckfastleigh, yeoman, William Luscombe Andrews of Broadhempston, yeoman, Luscombe William Andrews of Wheeldon, North Huish, yeoman, William Roope Ilbert of Bowringsleigh, West Alvington, esq., Frederick Trelawney Hare of Totnes, esq., Richard Andrews of Houghton, Bigbury, yeoman, John Adams Bartlett of Bidlake, Bridestowe gent., James Salter Bartlett of Ilsham, St

Marychurch, gent., John Manning of Washbourne, Ashprington, yeoman, Barnabas Tuckeman Green of Brixham, shipowner, and Frederick James Cornish Bowden of Blackhall, esq., trustees

2. Richard Evens of Diptford, yeoman

Premises: all that farm and estate called Blakewell containing fifty eight acres

Rent: £70

[3095 A - 1/PF 20 1877 Devon Record Office]

17 April 1877

Description Name Winsor, James

Official Number: 282720

Place of Birth: Bigbury near Kingsbridge, Devon

Dept Records of the Admiralty, Naval Forces, Royal Marines, Coastguard, and related bodies

Series Admiralty: Royal Navy Registers of Seamen's Services

Piece 282501-283000

[Catalogue reference ADM 188/452]

02 April 1877

Description Name Taylor, James

Official Number: 283560

Place of Birth: Bigbury, Devon

Dept Records of the Admiralty, Naval Forces, Royal Marines, Coastguard, and related bodies

Series Admiralty: Royal Navy Registers of Seamen's Services

Piece 283501-284000

[Catalogue reference ADM 188/454]

1878

Duke and Dowager Duchess of Cleveland own the manor. They and J A Pearse Esquire are the principal owners of the soil.

Parishes of Bigbury, Ringmore and Kingston now constitute the Erme & Avon School Board District

School Board includes:

Reverend F Farrer, J Wroth, W S Wroth, John White, P Randle, William Tidston, William Hooppell and F M Farrer [Clerk]

[Cookworthy Museum Village Notes]

Edward Wroth, farmer, occupies Court Buton Estate.

Thomas Gard - Farmer, High Cumery & victualler in Modbury

Joseph Foot - Victualler and shoemaker

Crimp - Farmer, Tuffland

Jeffery White - Farmer, Noddon farm; saddler in Modbury

The fishing rights at the mouth of the Avon belong to the Lord of the Manor, but are rented by John Ellis Esquire of Aveton Gifford.

John Amm - Parish Clerk

Bardqns Bros. (Joseph and Simon) - Fishing Boat Props md Pilots, The Warren

John Coker - Shoemaker

Frank Farren - Clerk to Erme & Avon School Board

John Hancock - Farmer and carrier

Harry Perraton - Farmer

Nicholas Roach - Shopkeeper and carrier

George Steer - Carpenter and shopkeeper

John Steer - Shopkeeper

Thomas Steer - Wheelwright

George Terry - Sexton and mason

Robert Terry - Mason

James Wakeham - Potato grower, New Quay

[Cookworthy Museum Village Notes]

1878-1892

Lease, Surrender and Letting

Houghton

Prettyjohn, Pearse, Andrew

[Agreement 1399M/3/4 1878 - 1892 Devon Record Office]

19 April 1878

Description Name Pearce, George

Official Number: 176079

Place of Birth: Bigbury, Devon

Dept Records of the Admiralty, Naval Forces, Royal Marines, Coastguard, and related bodies

Series Admiralty: Royal Navy Registers of Seamen's Services

Piece 176001-176500

[Catalogue reference ADM 188/290]

25 April 1879

Description Name Pengilly, Christopher John Roach

Official Number: 356284

Place of Birth: Bigbury, Devon

Dept Records of the Admiralty, Naval Forces, Royal Marines, Coastguard, and related bodies

Series Admiralty: Royal Navy Registers of Seamen's Services

Piece 356001-356500

[Catalogue reference ADM 188/539]

03 August 1879

Description Name Burgoyne, Frederick James

Official Number: 192333

Place of Birth: Bigbury, Devon

Dept Records of the Admiralty, Naval Forces, Royal Marines, Coastguard, and related bodies

Series Admiralty: Royal Navy Registers of Seamen's Services

Piece 192001-192400

[Catalogue reference ADM 188/329]

18 December 1879

Description Name Kingston, John Richard

Official Number: 188007

Place of Birth: Bigbury, Devon

Dept Records of the Admiralty, Naval Forces, Royal Marines, Coastguard, and related bodies

Series Admiralty: Royal Navy Registers of Seamen's Services

Piece 188001-188400

[Catalogue reference ADM 188/319]

06 January 1881

Description Name Lugger, Fredrick Disten

Official Number: 189623

Place of Birth: Bigbury, Devon

Dept Records of the Admiralty, Naval Forces, Royal Marines, Coastguard, and related bodies

Series Admiralty: Royal Navy Registers of Seamen's Services

Piece 189601-190000

[Catalogue reference ADM 188/323]

1884

Frogland Farm transferred from Kingston Parish to Bigbury Parish

26 September 1885

Description Name Hingston, Sydney

Official Number: 306670

Place of Birth: Bigbury, Devon

Dept Records of the Admiralty, Naval Forces, Royal Marines, Coastguard, and related bodies

Series Admiralty: Royal Navy Registers of Seamen's Services

Piece 306501-307000

[Catalogue reference ADM 188/500]

11 December 1885

Description Name Rendle, William Henry

Official Number: 306231

Place of Birth: Bigbury, Devon

Dept Records of the Admiralty, Naval Forces, Royal Marines, Coastguard, and related bodies

Series Admiralty: Royal Navy Registers of Seamen's Services

Piece 306001-306500

[Catalogue reference ADM 188/499]

1887

Edward Chatterton Orpen is Rector of Bigbury Parish Church

1889

Duke of Cleveland & Earl of Sandwich own the manor. J Wroth & the representatives of the late J A Pearse are the principal landowners.

Average attendance at school is 67 pupils. Lombard Jones is the master; Mrs Jones is Mistress.

Richard Crocker - Farmer, Houghton Estate

Garland Cuming - Farmer, Cumery

Arundel Crimp - Farmer, Tuffland; assessor & Tax Collector

Joseph Foot - Victualler of the Royal Oak Inn

John Hoddy - Farmer, Nodden Farm

John Wroth - Knowell Farm

Edward Chatterton Orpen - Rector

John Amm - Parish Clerk and blacksmith

John Coker - Shoemaker

Philip Hingston - Shoemaker

Nicholas Roach-Shopkeeper and farmer and carrier

John Steer - Shopkeeper

Thomas Steer - Carpenter and wheelwright

Robert Terry - Mason

James Wakeham – Butcher

[Coolworthy Museum Village Notes]

1894

Easton, also Dukes Mill Meadow parish

Aveton Gifford

Prettyjohn to Camp

[Lease 1399M/3/5 1894 Devon Record Office]

1895

First hotel built on Burgh Island by George Chirgwin.

1900

Receipt - work done on bells

[2925 A/PW 1 1900]

1908

Papers - work done on bells

[2925 A/PW 2 1908]

1904

Harold Bowden-Smith is Rector of Bigbury Parish Church

07 Jun 1904

THE BOLTON ESTATE, DEVON AND CORNWALL

1 Sale particulars (General/ordinary paper)

Court Farm, Bigbury, Devon

Coach House, Court Farm, Bigbury, Devon

Stables, Court Farm, Bigbury, Devon

Pilchard Inn, Burgh Island, Bigbury, Devon

Folly Farm, Bigbury, Devon

Hexdown Farm, Bigbury, Devon

Royal Oak, Bigbury, Devon

Dukes Mill, Bigbury, Devon

Rectory, Bigbury, Devon

Coach House, Rectory, Bigbury, Devon

Stables, Rectory, Bigbury, Devon

Tuffland Farm, Bigbury, Devon

Lower Cumery Farm, Cumery, Bigbury, Devon

Higher Cumery Farm, Cumery, Bigbury, Devon

Smithans and Boarshill Farm, Bigbury, Devon

[SC00227 English Heritage National Monuments Record]

Bigbury Bay, licence for drain for Mr W Balkwill

[The National Archives CRES 37/773]

1906-1934

Redemption of land tax for the parish of Bigbury, Devon (with detail from 1799)

With plans of pieces of land near Sedgewell Cove, pieces of land part of Folly Farm, land between Marine Drive and Parker Road, land near St Ann's Chapel

[114/3/59 1906-1934 Plymouth and West Devon Record Office]

1914

CONVEYANCE and MORTGAGE

1 George Shellabeer of Plymouth, contractor, George Gentle Shellabear of Plymouth, contractor and Henry Hurrell of Plymouth, merchant

2 Stanley Roger Huggins of Plymouth, builder

3 Thomas Lowry of Plymouth, house decorator

4 Richard Sanders of Bigbury, Devon, retired farmer

[1267/33 a and b 1914 Plymouth and West Devon Record Office]

1914

Mrs Wroth, Nicholas Pitts & the Bigbury Bay Development Syndicate are the principal landowners.

Average attendance at school is 36 prupils. Mrs Laura L Bastin is Mistress.

Alfred Douglas Bardens occupies the Royal Oak Inn

William Kerswell - Farmer, Houghton Estate

Edgar Peter Biddick - Farmer, Lower Cumery

Chales Rickman - Farmer, Higb Cumery

John Arundel Crimp - Farmer, Tuffland

George Harry Shepherd senior - Farmer, Noddon Farm

Augustus Luckcraft junior - Farmer, Frogland

C W Shepherd - Constable

Miss Kate Amm - Shopkeeper and sub-postmistress

Mrs Christina Badens – Refreshment rooms, Warren Cottage

Albert Hancock - Farmer

George Harry Shepherd junior - Farmer

John Steer – Wheelwright

1915

Alston in Malborough, Idestone in Aveton Gifford, Easton in Bigbury, and Chantry in Aveton Gifford

Pearse trustees to Pitts exors.

[1399M/8/3 1915 Devon Record Office]

16 September 1915

Conditions of sale and plans of Whympston estates and lands in Aveton Gifford, Bigbury, Loddiswell, Malborough and Modbury

[442/1-2 16 September 1915 Plymouth and West Devon Record Office]

1919

Sale particulars of Tuffland and Holwell, Bigbury, and Woodland Farm, Eggbuckland.

[442/3 12 June 1919 Plymouth and West Devon Record Office]

1924

Arthur Robert William Law is the Rector for Bigbury Parish Church

1926

Many bungalows erected here for summer visitors. GWR run a motor car service between Bigbury and Modbury daily.

May Brothers - Farmers, Houghton Estate

Chales Garland Rickman - Farmer, High Cumery

Walter Arundel Crimp - Farmer, Tufland

William Withycombe - Farmer, Frogland

John Stanley Wroth - Farmer, Knowle Farm

Mrs Laura L Bastin - School Mistress

Arthur Robert William Law - Rector

Mss Kate Amm - Sub-postmistress

Frank Leopold Wilhm Quires - Constable

John Steer - Wheelwright

Mrs Lily Bardens - Landlady of the Royal Oak Inn

1929

Burgh Island Hotel Built by Archibald Nettlefold

1929-1930

Papers re Messrs May Bros, land at St Anne's Chapel, Bigbury, Devon

With plan

[114/106 1929-1930 Plymouth and West Devon Record Office]

1929-1931

Papers re sale of land at Houghton and Cockle in parish of Bigbury, Devon

With plan

[114/176 1929-1931 Plymouth and West Devon Record Office]

1933

Charles Henry Pearn to Mrs Kate Roach, papers re sale and mortgage of a bungalow known as 'Gorton', Bigbury, Devon

[114/49/40 1933 Plymouth and West Devon Record Office]

1933

W E Blakenay, esq, agents letters regarding properties including the Fox & Hounds Hotel, Bridestowe, Devon; Pickwick Inn, Bigbury, Devon; Journey's End Hotel, Ringmore, Bigbury, Devon

[114/20/33 1933 Plymouth and West Devon Record Office]

1933

Land tax redemption office, miscellaneous correspondence, including references to Benjamin Hoopell, deceased, of Bigbury parish

[114/3/71 1933-1937 Plymouth and West Devon Record Office]

1935

William Jonathan May, Miss Mildred Alice May & Mrs Florence Harriet Popplestone to Mr H Bartlett, papers re sale of land called Great Church Park at Bigbury, Devon

[114/42/30 1935 Plymouth and West Devon Record Office]

1935

William Jonathan May, Mildred Alice May & Florence Harriet Popplestone to William Warren, sale of land known as Great Church Park, together with the right to draw water for household and domestic purposes, at Bigbury, Devon

[114/41/2 1935 Plymouth and West Devon Record Office]

1936

Mr William Jonathan May to Thomas George Woodmason, part of Great Church Park at Bigbury, Devon

With plan

[114/41/32 1936 Plymouth and West Devon Record Office]

1936

Mr William Jonathan May to William John Burgoyne, sale of land at Bigbury, Devon

With plan

[114/48/32 1936 Plymouth and West Devon Record Office]

1938

Papers re land and premises called 'Clee', Bigbury, South Devon, Messrs James William Camp Scoble & William James Scoble and Mrs Hilda Beatrice Pearn

[114/51/29 1938 Plymouth and West Devon Record Office]

1940

Mrs Sophie Annie Sanders to Thomas Arthur Pearn, draft receipt and other papers concerning 'Clee', Bigbury, Devon

[114/43/15 1940 Plymouth and West Devon Record Office]

1940

Mr William Jonathan May and Mrs Florence Harriet Popplestone, sale of land at St Anns Chapel, near Bigbury, Devon, for siting a new reservoir for Salcombe Water Board with other related papers

[114/48/40 1940 Plymouth and West Devon Record Office]

1942
Burgh Island Hotel bombed. Tower is destroyed.

About the Author

Jason D C Sullock is a member of the Devon Family History Society, and has been researching his family history for over twenty years.

He is the editor of several other Devon family history books and booklets, including:

Tin Miners of Devon

Farms of the South HamsMarket

Devon against the Armada

Dartmouth & the 1389 Poll Tax

Reprint of Arthur Mee's 'The King's England - Devon'

He is also the author of:

555 Quick n Dirty Marketing Tips

(These are currently being brought up-to-date and placed on www.lulu.com and www.amazon.com as both books and ebooks)

He lives on Teesside in the north-east of England, with his partner, Linda.

ADAMS, 29, 32, 33, 34, 48, 52, 53, 58, 59, 68, 73, 76, 105, 109, 114, 123

ALGAR, 68

ALLERY, 84

AMM, 72, 109, 125, 129, 131, 132

ANDREWS, 79, 108, 109, 123

ANN, 16, 64, 69, 70, 79, 84, 85, 86, 87, 88, 89, 90, 91, 92, 95, 96, 97, 98, 99, 100, 101, 102, 119

ANNE, 15, 81

ANTHONY, 16, 23, 26, 43, 61

ARUNDEL, 5, 128, 131, 132

ASFORD, 7

AVENT, 35, 38, 40, 41, 44, 62

AVENTS, 40, 57

BACHYLER, 10

BALDWYN, 18

BALKWILL, 130

BALPATCHETT, 85

BARDEN, 61

BARDENS, 35, 37, 39, 41, 42, 44, 45, 46, 47, 48, 49, 50, 51, 53, 55, 56, 57, 60, 62, 83, 88, 108, 109, 114, 120, 131, 132

BARDON, 85

BARDONS, 37, 43, 51, 59, 67

BARNES, 62, 123

BARTLETT, 109, 123, 133

BASETT, 71

BASSETT, 75

BASTARD, 23, 31

BASTIN, 131, 132

BEAR, 112

BEARD, 109, 112

BEARE, 32

BEAVLE, 86

BECK, 105, 109, 114

BEER, 109, 113

BEKEBYR, 8

BEVELL, 39

BEWES, 106

BICKHAM, 87

BIDDICK, 131

BIGBERIE, 13

BIGBURY, 1, 3, 4, 5, 6, 7, 8, 9, 10, 13, 14, 15, 16, 17, 19, 20, 22, 23, 24, 25, 26, 27, 28, 29, 30, 31, 32, 33, 34, 37, 38, 39, 40, 41, 42, 43, 44, 46, 47, 48, 49, 50, 51, 52, 53, 54, 55, 56, 57, 58, 59, 60, 61, 63, 64, 66, 67, 68, 69, 70, 71, 72, 73, 74, 75, 76, 77, 78, 79, 80, 81, 82, 83, 84, 104, 106, 107, 108, 111, 112, 113, 114, 115, 116, 117, 118, 119, 120, 121, 122, 123, 124, 126, 127, 128, 129, 130, 131, 132, 133, 134

BIKABERY, 6

BIKBURY, 14

BIKBY, 14

BIKEBURI, 8, 9

BIRD, 78

BISCOE, 56

BLACKER, 50

BLACKLER, 39, 41, 42, 44, 48, 51, 56, 62

BLACKLOR, 40

BLAKENAY, 133

BLOUNT, 15

BLUNT, 16

BOICS, 10

BOON, 87

BORRETT, 56

BORRYER, 65

BOWDEN, 18, 124, 129

BOYLAND, 7

BOYS, 7

BREND, 50, 62, 70, 109

BREWES, 8

BROCKINGTON, 105

BROKE, 14, 15

BROOKE, 16

BROOKING, 30

BROWN, 109, 111, 117, 119

BUNKER, 118, 121

BURGOYNE, 127, 134

BURLEIGH, 20

BURLEY, 17, 68, 109

BURWOOD, 21

BUTLAND, 123

BYEBURY, 7

BYKBURY, 14

BYKEBIRI, 7

BYKEBUR, 7

BYKEBURY, 8, 10, 11, 12

BYLHOLE, 11, 12

BYTTE, 18

CARY, 34

CAWLEY, 19

CHAMBERNON, 9

CHAMBERNOU, 10

CHAMPENOWNES, 4

CHAMPERNON, 14

CHAMPERNOUN, 11, 12

CHAMPERNOWN, 13

CHAMPERNOWNES, 6, 13

CHARLES II, 30

CHEVERSTONE, 9

CHIDDERLEGH, 10

CHIPMAN, 74

CHIRGWIN, 129

CHISMIN, 33

CHMPERNOWNE, 36

CHOLDWILTH, 61

CHUBB, 64

CHUDERLEGH, 11

CLARKE, 24

CLYFF, 17

COAD, 78

COAKER, 108

COCKER, 41, 80, 90, 108, 109, 112, 114

COFFIN, 27

COKER, 41, 75, 125, 129

COLE, 14, 23, 72, 88, 105, 109, 111, 114

3

COLTON, 46, 47, 48, 50

COMEROY, 78

COOKE, 18, 36

CORBYN, 9

CORKER, 75

CORNISH, 34, 43, 57, 61, 67, 124

CORY, 31

COSTERD, 20

COUCH, 72, 76, 79, 109

COULTON, 65, 66, 67

COUNTESS DOWAGER OF BATH, 30

COURTICE, 30

COVE, 61, 130

COWKEER, 21

COWKER, 22

COYTE, 18, 21, 69, 70

CRANCH, 31, 32, 35, 41, 61, 68

CREER, 65

CRIMP, 125, 128, 131, 132

CROCKER, 66, 80, 106, 109, 114, 117, 128

CROUCH, 89

CUMBE, 9

CUMING, 78, 108, 109, 128

CUMMING, 109

CUNNING, 78

DAVIE, 66

DAVIS, 82, 117

DAW, 89

DAWE, 81

DAWTREY, 15

DAWTREYS, 15

DERRY, 104

DINGLE, 62, 68, 71, 83, 105, 109, 114

DOLTON, 89

DRAKE, 10, 14, 17

DUCHESS OF CLEVELAND, 4, 124

DUKE OF BOLTON, 37, 38, 40, 41, 42, 43, 44, 80

DUKE OF BOULTON, 54

DUKE OF CLEVELAND, 4, 5, 105, 108, 128

DURNEFORD, 14

DURNFORD, 13

DYER, 55, 56

DYMME, 12

DYMMOK, 11

DYNHAM, 13, 14

EARL OF BOLTON, 39

EDGCOMBE, 29, 39

EDWARDS, 42

EGGECOMB, 14

EILIOT, 39

ELBERT, 61

ELIOT, 81

ELIOTT, 43, 45, 46, 56

ELLARE, 46

ELLERT, 47

ELLIOT, 34, 36, 37, 38, 39, 40, 62, 70, 74, 81

ELLIOTT, 40, 41, 42, 44, 45, 47, 48, 49, 50, 51, 53, 54, 55, 57, 58, 59, 60, 62, 63, 65, 69, 72, 73, 74, 76, 79

ELLIOTTS, 53, 61

ELLIS, 4, 61, 73, 125

ELLYOTT, 18

ELWORTHY, 90

EVENS, 124

FANE, 63

FARLY, 90

FARREN, 125

FARRER, 5, 123, 125

FARWELL, 68, 76, 79

FERRERS, 10, 22, 76

FINNEY, 52

FLETCHER, 90

FOALE, 90

FOLEFORD, 10, 11

FOOT, 64, 67, 68, 82, 108, 109, 111, 123, 125, 128

FORD, 66, 89, 109, 112

FORDE, 18

FORTESCU, 10

FORTESCUE, 29, 30, 57, 108

FOSS, 123

FOX, 6, 81, 105, 109, 133

FREEMAN, 91

FRIEND, 80, 109

FROOD, 35

FROST, 91

FROUDE, 91

FULL, 91

FURLONG, 75

FURNEAUX, 123

FURSE, 26

FURZEMAN, 91

GAMBON, 10, 11, 12

GARD, 125

GARD, 91

GEE, 64

GEECH, 36

GEORGE, 18, 22, 23, 29, 36, 40, 49, 50, 65, 70, 72, 73, 80, 82, 84, 85, 86, 87, 88, 89, 90, 91, 92, 96, 97, 98, 100, 102, 105, 106, 111, 119, 123, 125, 126, 129, 131, 134

GERMAN, 91

GEST, 30

GETSIUS, 29, 30

GILBERD, 24, 36

GILBERT, 13, 30, 100

GILES, 8, 18

GILL, 17, 105, 109, 114

GILLARD, 20, 109

GIST, 91

GLUBB, 64

GOODMAN, 109, 119, 120, 122

GORGEIS, 12

GOSS, 27, 71, 77, 78

GRANT, 9, 10, 12, 109

GREEN, 124

GREVILLE, 15

HUST, 22

HUXTABLE, 93

HYDESTON, 10

ILBERT, 68, 123

JACKSON, 31, 32, 123

JAGO, 29, 106

JANE, 14, 18, 81, 84, 85, 86, 87,
88, 90, 91, 92, 94, 95, 97, 98,
99, 100, 101, 103, 104, 108,
114, 117

JAUNE, 9

JEFFERY, 93

JOHNS, 80

JOHNSON, 123

JOLLE, 18

JONES, 128

JOSEPH, 23, 31, 40, 44, 56, 74,
77, 85, 86, 87, 89, 90, 91, 94,
114, 123, 125, 128

JUDD, 9

JUDDE, 10

KEETT, 43, 45

KERSWELL, 59, 70, 71, 131

KING, 6, 13, 27, 32, 33, 35, 43,
45, 52, 55, 62

KING DINGLE, 52

KINGDINGLE, 50, 58

KINGSTON, 5, 8, 22, 30, 57,
65, 124, 127

KIRKHAM, 29

KIT, 39, 64

KITT, 20, 34, 35, 37, 40, 43, 44,
47, 49, 51, 58, 59, 60, 61, 62,
65, 66, 110

KITTE, 18

KNAPMAN, 69

KNOWLES, 105

LAKE, 68, 80

LAKEMAN, 43, 49

LAMB, 66

LAMBELL, 68

LAMBORNE, 63

LANE, 69, 108, 110, 122

LANG, 27, 81, 84

LANGMEAD, 84

LANGWORTHY, 33

LAPTHORN, 94

LARKMAN, 42

LASKEY, 31

LAVERS, 23, 110

LAW, 132

LAWRENCE, 94

LEAR, 94

LEE, 39, 49, 50, 51, 54, 55, 57,
60, 62, 64, 72, 108

LEES, 47

LEGASSICK, 94

LEGASSICKE, 68, 76

LEIGE, 94

LEIGH, 17, 33, 35, 37, 40, 41,
44, 110

LEIGHE, 41

LEVY, 94

UPPETON, 12

VALLETORTA, 6

VEALE, 27, 64

VOISEY, 102

WAKEHAM, 18, 33, 34, 35, 40,
57, 62, 70, 71, 75, 111, 112,
114, 115, 123, 125, 129

WARD, 102

WARDEN, 102

WARREN, 26, 90, 100, 125,
131, 134

WARTHE, 12

WATTS, 78

WAY, 24

WEBB, 102

WEBBER, 18, 38, 50, 62

WENTHE, 11

WERTHA, 12

WHAKEAM, 103

WHAKEHAM, 102, 103

WHAKHAM, 103

WHIDON, 59

WHITCHAIR, 70

WHITCHILL, 22

WHITE, 5, 50, 58, 71, 76, 125

WHITELL, 75

WIDGER, 116

WILLING, 35, 36, 37, 41, 42,
43, 44, 47, 48, 50, 54, 55, 56,
57, 60, 62, 64, 66

WILLINGE, 18, 21

WILLINGS, 38, 105, 114, 123

WILLOUGHBY, 14, 15

WILLOUGHBYS, 4, 13

WILLS, 106

WILTON, 14, 106, 111, 113

WINN, 70

WINSLAND, 103

WINSOR, 124

WINTER, 103

WITHYCOMBE, 132

WOLFS, 8

WOOD, 25, 28, 30, 119

WOODMASON, 28, 45, 67, 68,
83, 108, 111, 114, 134

WOOLDRIDGE, 74

WOOLLCOMBE, 31, 32

WOOLLRIDGE, 51

WOOLRIDGE, 48

WOTTON, 35, 47

WROTH, 5, 80, 104, 105, 108,
111, 113, 114, 123, 125, 128,
129, 131, 132

WYLLOUGHBY, 16

WYLUGHBY, 16

WYRTHE, 10

YEARELL, 21

YELLINGE, 21

2865007R00075

Printed in Great Britain
by Amazon.co.uk, Ltd.,
Marston Gate.